D0723291

Publisher's Lunch

PUBLISHER'S LUNCH

A DIALOGUE

Concerning the Secrets of
How Publishers Think & What
Authors Can Do About It

Ernest Callenbach

TEN SPEED PRESS
Berkeley, California

Copyright © 1989 by Ernest Callenbach

All rights reserved. No part of this book may be reproduced
in any form, except for brief reviews, without the written
permission of the publisher.

TEN SPEED PRESS
P.O. Box 7123
Berkeley, CA 94707

Library of Congress Cataloging-in-Publication Data

Callenbach, Ernest.
Publisher's lunch.

Bibliography: p.
Includes index.
1. Imaginary conversations.   2. Authors and publishers.
3. Publishers and publishing.   I. Title.
PS3553.A424P84   1989   813'.54   88-29646
ISBN 0-89815-288-7
ISBN 0-89815-287-9 (pbk.)

Printed in the United States of America

1 2 3 4 5 - 93 92 91 90 89

TO

All authors whose work has been rejected
but will someday prove wildly popular

TO

All publishers who sometimes issue books they love
but know in their hearts will not sell

TO

All agents who cosset arrogant authors
whose talent outweighs their ingratitude

TO

All booksellers who remember that they deal
in precious contacts between souls

TO

All bold readers who buy unhyped books
from small publishers and unknown authors

AND TO

All those who want to be authors or publishers
but don't know what they're getting into

1

MENU ONE

Martini Cocktail   White Wine
Pizzetta with Tapenade & Mozzarella
Fried Softshell Crabs with Mayonnaise
Risotto of Quail & Morels
Shrimp Fettucine
Green Salad with Vinaigrette Dressing
Strawberry-Tangerine Granita

J: Excuse me—are you Michelle?

M: Jim! You haven't changed a bit!

J: Well, *you* have. I mean . . .

M: Come on over here—they've reserved my special table. Toss your manuscript on that chair. Welcome to the restaurant where I bring particularly promising authors. I thought my favorite professor deserved the same treatment.

J: I'm flattered. Just let me get collected here. I . . . well, I can't get used to how you look. So elegant! Do you mind if I stare a minute?

M: Go ahead. I used to stare at you plenty during your lectures. Turn about's fair play.

J: Your hair's so short! Very businesslike. And your face seems narrower than I remember, or sharper angles or something. It's more dramatic. But the same smiling brown eyes.

M: A few little wrinkles in the corners?

J: Yes. You're not a kid any more. Somehow I hadn't really registered that over the phone. God, what a lucky phone call! The really odd thing is that during the past couple of months you've been popping into my mind a lot. In fact last week I ran up to a woman on campus who was wearing a vest sweater like your old green one. It wasn't you, of course. But now here you are.

M: Well, I wouldn't have predicted you'd ever think of me again, actually. How did you come to call our office, anyway? Did you find Terra Press listed in the *Literary Market Place* or something?

J: No. It was just one of those accidents. I was telling a colleague how my manuscript had been turned down by seven New York publishers so far, and he mentioned that he was reading something Terra had published. About the ecological side of the troubles in Central America . . . I forget the author's name.

M: That's one of my books!

J: Well, he thought it was so original that he was surprised a commercial house had done it. That made him think Terra might be interested in my offbeat project too. And then your familiar voice came on the line. —Has it actually been twelve years?

M: Impossible, just look at you! Maybe there's a little more grey in your beard, but you're as lean as ever.

J: I still pace around in the classroom a lot. And remember how spread out the campus is. I dig compost into my garden. I chop wood, trying to keep up with the rural life. So it's always a good change to get in to town.

M: How strange it is to see you! I wasn't sure I could handle this, Jim. I'm still not sure.

J: You know, martinis may be out of fashion, but I'm going

to have one anyway. Just to keep one old publishing tradition alive, anyway. Join me?

M: Of course. I love martinis.

J: I don't want to make things difficult, Michelle. I was just going to keep trying this brainchild of mine on more publishers, and see what happens. But I could sure use some advice.

M: I want to try to help, Jim. After all, twelve years ago is ancient history. And besides, whatever happened wasn't only your doing.

J: I just suddenly panicked about what a divorce would mean to my kids.

M: I guessed that. And I had to respect it, you know. I still do, though I felt horribly rejected. I wasn't eager to be a twenty-two-year-old stepmother, but still . . .

J: I knew it was awful for you, but I didn't see what I could do about it. After we—it was put up or shut up. So I shut up.

M: You might have returned a couple of my desperate phone calls.

J: I figured that would make everything worse.

M: Maybe. But you were the most fascinating man I'd ever met. I thought you understood everything! So I depended on you to know how far we could go. That wonderful weekend at the lake, I began to hope that we could somehow work out a way to be a couple, at least for a while. Then suddenly you weren't there any more, even to tell me to get lost.

J: I was paralyzed. And you know, a month hasn't gone by that I haven't been sorry for it.

M: Really? Maybe breaking that academic incest taboo was . . . well, we never know how fate is going to arrange things for us, do we? But now at least it offers us a civilized lunch. So I think we should just relax and enjoy it.

J: Yes. And I *am* enjoying it. This is my kind of restaurant —a big plain room, white tablecloths, simple china and silverware. Nothing to distract us from talking—and that was always a shared pleasure with no taboo on it.

M: The menu can be a little distracting. Look at this: risotto of quail and morels.

J: I was thinking of the fried softshell crabs with mayonnaise myself. Saving room for the strawberry-tangerine granita, of course.

M: Anyway, I bet you'll find the food almost worth what they charge for it.

J: I can believe that, from the garlicky smells! —I'm glad we're meeting here and not in your office. It must be full of shelves of manuscripts, waiting to be sent back to their anxious authors.

M: Waiting to be read, mostly.

J: Michelle, don't you want to take a quick look at my

manuscript before we eat? Maybe I should give you a little background about . . .

M: We'll get to it. After all these years you turn up again —I want to savor the moment! Besides, publishers' lunches are supposed to be leisurely.

J: I'll leisurely watch you sip that martini then. I can only remember you drinking mint tea. You used to like to slurp it. Then you'd lick your lips, very slowly.

M: That was because I put a lot of honey in it. I've stopped slurping, I assure you.

J: Nowadays students want capuccinos, so the caffeine impact will keep them going. It's harder now, being a student. It's almost as hard as the real world. But it looks like you've landed on your feet.

M: As long as I don't drink too many martinis, anyway. No—I'm one of the lucky ones. I found something I like to do, and even get paid for it. In some ways it's as varied as teaching.

J: Teaching still seems the only way to live, for me. Did I tell you on the phone that I got through all that toadying for tenure? So I can teach mostly the courses I want. And I have a fair amount of free time to do other things, like write unpublishable books.

M: Don't you have to publish papers?

J: I write an article every once in a while. My Faulkner book got me tenure. Then, when nobody paid much attention to that, I began thinking of writing things that *might* get some attention—even if they wouldn't help me rise through the academic ranks. So I wrote a popular book on family patterns through history, in literature and in life. A would-be popular book, actually.

M: It must have slipped by me somehow. What was it called?

J: *Families Past, Families Future.* You're forgiven—it slipped by almost everybody. I was trying to rehabilitate the family as a resource for the future and call for a rebirth of the extended family. After all, it's been the normal human living pattern for a hundred thousand years. I thought I addressed some really important issues that everybody has left to the rightwingers lately, about what we really need in the way of family. And then how we could get it without falling back into the old patriarchal patterns.

M: That should have stirred up some discussion!

J: It should have. It may be the best writing I ever did, though I'm fond of the new one too. But the publisher gave it a premature burial. So here I am, forty-four years old—I've had a lot of good times, but not a brilliant career so far. Oh, yes, and about two years ago Jan and I finally did get divorced.

M: Really? I heard a while back that you were still married.

J: Yeah. One reason I stuck it out so long was to help Jan find a way to make a living. And I felt I had to wait for the kids to get older. They were fifteen and seventeen when we split up.

M: I'm sure it was good for them that you stayed around.

I can't imagine them almost grown up. They live with Jan?

J: Mostly. They've turned out to be fine people. Sam's off to college—wants to study classics, bless him. I suspect he's inherited my tendency to hope that we can learn from the past. It's harder with Amy. We're really in tune on some levels, but right now she thinks life at my little house is hopelessly boring because I won't let her play her music at full power. They're both okay.

M: Are *you* okay, Jim?

J: Maybe you should give me your diagnosis at the end of lunch. Lately I've been looking back over my life and trying to change it a little, to tell you the truth. That's how this manuscript got started—I took a leave of absence, bought a secondhand Winnebago, and hit the road for six months. And then I fell in with these lively retired people out there in the desert, and decided there was a book in it.

M: "I want you to tell me the truth."

J: What? Oh, I used to say that to *you*, didn't I?

M: That telling the truth was what writing was about.

J: And you would always smile. Just the way you're smiling now.

M: Well, it touched me to think that writers could strive and suffer to tell the truth, no matter who they were or where they came from or what they were writing about. And that you and I could *see* this and know why it was important. Let the rest of the class go play tennis! It was thrilling to feel that we were together in a kind of conspiracy for the truth. And sometimes now I feel that about an author, and it warms my heart. —That's actually the most important thing I learned from you in all those courses.

J: Really? And then after we . . . well, I knew how hurt you were, but it would've been nice to hear from you after a while. Would you mind catching me up?

M: I had to move on, you know—not look back. So I went to Europe for the summer. But I was still at a loss what to do next, so I stayed with friends in New York who found me a job in a bookstore, at first just to be doing something. I got to know some publishers' sales reps, and then a couple of editors, and publishing looked more and more interesting.

M: I wouldn't have thought the glamor would get you. So what did?

J: It's *not* glamorous. Famous authors can be a pain in the ass, and a lot of it is hard, slogging office work. But I could see that editors have a certain autonomy, a bit like what you academics have. A chance to use your mind on something *you* decide is worth thinking about, at least part of the time. So that gave me an objective to shoot for.

J: Didn't you have to take courses or something, to get in the door?

M: No. I could type and make myself useful, so I was one of the lucky ones who get jobs as assistant to an editor and then ease their way into doing editorial work. After a while I brought off a couple of coups, and I started a series of health books that did well. So I began getting paid almost decently enough to afford New York. I stuck it out for five years. But when I was offered this job, I was glad to leave.

Now I can do some ecology books, which are my first love, and actually enjoy nature a little. So there you have it, a synopsis of my life.

J: More adventurous than mine, I'm afraid. I just kept on doing what I'd been doing. It was okay, but toward the end of my marriage it sometimes felt like life had taken a detour and left me in an emotional ghost town. And even the teaching went kind of dead on me for a while. I missed you, Michelle. Maybe you didn't realize it, but you were the only student who kept me totally awake. —You're still my favorite student, after all these years.

M: I am? That's . . . well, that's astonishing! I assume you're not just thinking of that weekend.

J: Cut it out. Like the song says, I touched your perfect body with my mind. What I really loved was that you were willing to let things *matter* to you—not grades, but reality. You had a certain . . . I don't know what to call it . . .

M: Arrogance? From having kicked my Catholic upbringing?

J: It just seemed like freedom. You were a fellow free spirit. And I envied you for being younger and freer!

M: I thought you had everything, knew everything, and could do everything. And you envied *me*?

J: Sure. You were right not to go on for a Ph. D. The process destroys the capacity for independent thought.

M: Then how come it didn't get you?

J: I'm more ornery than you are. I'm like a mule. I can

work in harness, I just kick a lot. You're . . . well, maybe your totem animal is the deer. Natural grace and surprising leaps and bounds.

M: Then you're a bear—cranky sometimes, but smart and independent. I used to love watching you knock over intellectual garbage cans. You're mischievous, too—you like to make trouble. Look at those sly little eyes!

J: Me? What are you talking about?

M: I know you, Jim. Once I even figured out why you always think bad news is more interesting than good—it produces livelier arguments.

J: You're right, there. Good news bores me, unless there's someone cheerful around to share it with. Like you.

M: Anyway, I knew I wasn't cut out for teaching. Though when you phoned the other day I did feel a twinge of guilt, as if I had let you down by leaving school.

J: You could absolve yourself by publishing *Home on the Road.*

M: If it deserves publishing I'll try to publish it. Just the way you used to give me an A if I deserved it.

J: And will your criteria be the same as mine, now that the tables are turned?—God, look at that cruel, cruel smile!

M: Sure. I'm after truth, beauty, organization, style, and power. Not to forget glory. And something you didn't have to grade me on, salability. Incidentally, what did those New York houses say when they rejected your manuscript?

M: Nothing of any use. "Doesn't fit our list," that crap. One was sort of interested but finally said it was too far out for them and why didn't I publish it myself to test the waters. Then if it started selling they might take it on. That's what first made me aware of the self-publishing possibility I wanted to ask you about. But of course it didn't improve my opinion of publishers. Why should authors take the initial financial risks and do their market research for them? I thought that was what publishers were for! Actually, I wouldn't have given either of my publishers much above C-minus, if that.

M: Publishing is different from academia. Academia is about power, publishing is about money.

J: But academics have no power!

M: Sure they do. Look at all that hierarchy business—the power of deans over chairs, and chairs over professors, and professors over assistant professors, and all professors over students, and . . .

J: Editors have power over authors, too.

M: We do have some, even if we're women—so long as we're good enough. But the power we have is narrowly constrained by money. It's a perilous business.

J: Then why have multinational corporations gobbled up so many publishing houses? I don't think I understand publishing at all. Is there a short course I could enroll in? "Self-Defense for Authors 103"?

M: You sound a bit bruised. Maybe I should give you the view from the other side.

J: How would I know whether you're telling me the truth?

M: You used to say that it could be deduced from the style. So you could sit there while I lecture, sipping your martini and doing stylistic analysis. But if you really want it, I promise you'll get the whole truth, maybe more than you want to know. Besides, I can see you're in trouble, and I happen to be in a position where I might be able to help.

J: I didn't know it was so obvious. All right. I'm a desperate author with life in picturesque ruins and a much-rejected manuscript which my friends tell me I had better start thinking about self-publishing. You're a kind-hearted publisher, which I'm willing to stipulate is not a contradiction in terms, and you're going to explain to me the secrets of the trade, everything I need to know to stave off high blood pressure and possibly bankruptcy.

M: I notice that the question of money has arisen, as it always soon does in publishing. Which reminds me we'd better settle something: how are we going to pay for the lunch? I take it this isn't the usual publisher's lunch, where I would be wooing you. And paying for the privilege.

J: No, we have to be equals. Neither of us can guess if you'll be interested in my manuscript, and maybe self-publication *will* be the way to go with it. I just need some disinterested advice, Michelle. So let's split the bill.

M: Agreed—clause number one. Incidentally, we have to get rid of this baguette, don't you think? It has a distinctly day-old feel to it. And I recommend we both indulge in their fettucine. It's glorious.

J: It's tempting, but then I'd have to pass up the pizzetta with tapenade and mozzarella.

M: Oh, I don't know. I'm hungry. Let's split a pizzetta. They don't use that diminutive loosely—we can handle it! They also have a surprisingly good house white wine.

J: Fine. If you like it, I'm sure I'll like it.—I'm beginning to feel this is an auspicious occasion!

M: Here's to it, then. Whatever "it" turns out to be.

J: In my new life, I'm trying to appreciate ambiguity.

M: Good, because ambiguity is a publisher's middle name. Now where shall we begin?

J: Will you tell me all about the high rollers and back stabbers in New York, and those million-dollar advances and movie deals?

M: No. First because I only move along the edges of that world myself, and second because you don't need to know about the rare lottery winners, at least not yet. You have to begin by learning how to handle yourself in the neighborhood poker game.

J: Then let's start with a list of my author friends' most horrendous complaints about their publishers.

M: I know them all already, unfortunately. Let's just begin at the beginning.

J: Okay, I have a manuscript . . .

M: No. If you want to know how publishers think, that's *not* the beginning. The beginning for us is that we have a publishing house. It can be a small privately owned firm, a cog in some giant international conglomerate, a university press, or an employee-owned firm. But the similarities are much greater than the differences.

J: It's just a dirty business?

M: A particularly crazy kind of business.

J: You're telling me!

M: Inhabited by some of the most devoted, hardest-trying people you'll ever meet. Then there are some bums and crooks. But all of us live within a relentless business context, and that's the single hardest thing for authors to grasp.

J: We should have a blackboard—I see points one through twenty coming up. Who said you shouldn't have gone into teaching? I'll have to pay close attention.

M: You'd better, because there's a test—called writing a contract.

J: Now wait . . .

M: I said "a" contract, not "your" contract. All I will admit to is the slightest gleam of the eye, a suspicion that inside that modest-looking box over there you just might have something fantastic.—Who's tempting who, here?

J: Tempting *whom.*

M: I'm the editor here, professor, and editors get to take

liberties. Now, in this country each year there are about sixty thousand books published, using a rather loose definition of "book." Even if that's a generous estimate, America is not a great reading country, compared to Japan or Britain, say. Even Spain publishes thirty thousand titles every year, with a population only one-seventh of ours.

J: Wait a minute. The Spaniards are reading almost four times as many books per person as we do? And still finding time for siestas?

M: That's titles, not copies. It's possible that our average book sells more copies per capita, though I doubt it. But they don't watch so much television. Worse yet, our sixty thousand books have to be sold to a limited market of book readers—because only a small fraction of Americans read any books at all. Sorry if "market" sounds crass. But the point is brutal and has to be faced. How many books a year do *you* buy?

J: I guess maybe . . . well, let's see, probably about a hundred. Yes, say two a week, maybe a little more, counting paperbacks. Of course I also use the library . . .

M: But that leaves fifty-nine thousand nine hundred books out there of which you, not to mention most of your friends, have not bought any copies. *Every year.* And if you really do buy a hundred a year you're an outstandingly regular customer. What I'm saying is that the publishing business has a case of chronic overproduction. The closest parallel is farming. And you know what's been happening to farmers —especially small farmers.

J: Well, if the government won't bail you out, why don't

all you publishers get together and cut down on your production, then?

M: There are antitrust laws . . .

J: Watch it, you promised to tell the truth.

M: Okay, the real reason is that short of some kind of cabal, it appears to be in the short-term interest of every firm to publish a lot of books. Except for cookbooks and maybe formula romance novels, each book represents a largely unknown risk. This is very exciting—you get paid to gamble with other people's money.

J: I remember you once thinking you ought to get into something physically risky, like hang-gliding. But you never showed any signs of being a gambler.

M: Maybe not then, but that's a big part of why I'm in publishing. It truly rivets your attention to have to decide whether to spend forty thousand dollars on something that could hit big, and then again could be a total disaster! And I seem to have a good commercial nose. It's not brains, you know.

J: And not just luck?

M: That helps, but there's also some kind of off-center perception involved. Good editors sort of half-consciously notice something about manuscripts that most people miss. And they find the courage to go for them. Of course you also do all the rational calculating you can, by looking at comparable books, talking to people with more experience, trying to be sharp, and that's exciting in another way.

J: But it doesn't stop you from doing too many books. By the way, you were right—the fettucine is luscious. And they're generous with the shrimp.

M: I'm glad you're happy with it! Now how about some salad to offset the creamy stuff? Editors get very hungry, maybe because we burn up so much energy trying to be productive.

J: Do you have a quota to meet?

M: No, but if we only brought in that one perfect book each year, we wouldn't last long. Besides, there's the factor that any decent new manuscript can look very enticing, and you figure there must be room for one more. Taking a lot of risks somehow seems more likely to result in an occasional smash. Which pays for the losses on the other books.

J: You couldn't pass elementary statistics believing that. It's just superstition—one more bet on one more horse, and the odds must get better.

M: But it's appealing all the same, even if you remember the old rule of thumb that only one of every seven titles makes money. And some publishers also deliberately publish occasional books at prices they know will lose money, figuring to recoup it later through reprints, or income from paperback rights or movies and television, or translations. Which may happen sometimes.

J: Don't your bankers stop you, or the Germans or Brits or whoever owns your company now? Stop giving you capital to print books?

M: If our bets don't pay off over time, sure. But with luck it can be a long time.

J: It all sounds highly irrational. Maybe even irresponsible.

M: I'd never raise any daughter of mine to be a publisher.

J: You have a daughter? You didn't say you were married. Or had been—I notice you don't wear a ring.

M: I haven't been married. Books have been my children.

J: Hmm. Well, can't publishers exercise birth control? The fact that there are too many books must hurt authors, publishers, investors, bookstores, everybody.

M: Except maybe readers. But don't forget the overproduction of manuscripts by authors. Can you *imagine* what it's like to face the fact that every day of your life, hundreds of thousands of manuscripts, most of them totally worthless, are pouring out of every city and town in this giant country? And that lots of them are going to come crashing onto your desk?

J: So you exercise benevolent triage, or expect agents to do it for you.

M: Not always so benevolent. An editor can't expect to be loved, only respected. And that's not easy. My rejection letters started out as four pages of single-spaced hand-wringing and advice. Now they're down to a kindly, vague paragraph.

J: Does that help authors feel better?

M: Of course not, nothing helps. This is real life, "history." History is what hurts, somebody said.

J: An author, I'll bet.

M: Of course. God bless authors. I'm certainly not one of those publishers who'd like to see authors replaced by computers! Well, anyway: how could one publisher find the point of entry to begin changing the vicious circle? Sure, I could tell authors that we have too many books signed up already, and can't take theirs on. We could say that to a lot of authors, cut the size of our seasonal lists by a quarter, fire a quarter of our staff—thus ending a lot of pleasant lunches . . .

J: Then I'm against it.

M: And besides, unless everybody did it, the result would simply be that we would shrink and a couple of other firms would expand.

J: So it wouldn't even save trees or result in the publication of less junk.

M: You can also argue that some degree of overproduction serves the whole society best. If we publish somewhat too many books, fewer authors get left out, fewer interests go unserved, fewer ideas get lost.

J: So the fact that publishers as a group behave self-destructively is cause for rejoicing? Publishing so many books that most authors get short-changed and live lives of unholy poverty is supposed to be good for the intellectual health of the country?

M: It's foolish but noble. Suppose your ideas or style happen to be unorthodox and likely to be unprofitable. Then only a few publishers would dare to consider your manuscript seriously. And you might find it very noble indeed that they wanted to publish a few more books, so long as one of them was yours.

J: But I keep reading that the golden age of daring publishers is over. Look at publishing offices—they're infested with accountants and their computers! Editors jump from publisher to publisher like fleas! There's no loyalty, no trust between authors and publishers anymore . . .

M: Calm down, you'll choke on your lettuce. Authors and publishers have *always* been wary of each other, for perfectly sound reasons. It's like insurers and insurees. Each side is essential to the other—and also the other's chief problem.

J: But publishing back in the twenties and thirties used to be a gentlemanly profession. Publishers took care of their authors!

M: Don't kid yourself, Jim. It was a business then and it's a business now. Besides, aren't authors in business too? When writers get together, how often do you find them discussing literary technique and new trends in the fictional arts? They talk about money and deals and status and power, like most people. They have accountants too, and a guild and even a union. As far as loyalty goes—well, a lot of authors are glad to snatch work or glory away from other people if they get the slightest chance.

J: *Some* authors are noble creatures, selfless and pure. Even if we do have a few flaws, without us there'd be nothing to publish. We're where the ideas come from. It's our yearning fingers that put all those wonderful little marks down on paper!

M: Right, and *now* we finally get to your manuscript. It may be full of brilliant ideas, stylishly written, and represent ten years of agony for you. Your editor has presumably shown great enthusiasm about it. But then the manuscript goes into the production process and for the people within the publishing house it becomes just another book.

J: That's what a poet friend of mine used to complain about. He said most publishers might as well be selling tires.

M: Yes, and I bet he imagined it's easier to sell books than tires. He should have tried it some time! What I meant is that if a book is going to get published, it has to go through the same stages as other books. It must take on a physical and financial identity, which means a budget. Somehow, detailed calculations have to be made about how much the book will cost to publish, and how much it can be expected to bring back in income. It would help if authors kept this in mind when they're making their non-negotiable demands.

J: I can see it now: a tiny little figure, "royalties," balanced against a great big one, "profits."

M: In actual fact, often the better the book, the smaller the profits. A wise old publisher once said that either a book should be good, or it should sell.—Lord, how can it have gotten so late? Another author is coming to the office in fifteen minutes.

J: Are you still charmingly forgetful, the way you used to be about returning library books?

M: I didn't forget, I just didn't want to give them up. And now I'm a creature of my schedule. I'm truly sorry, Jim. We have a lot more to talk about, don't we?

J: And we've held up under the strain—or have we?

M: Much better than I expected! It's been good to see you again, really it has. And I promise to look at your manuscript in the next few days and get back to you about it.

J: Look, why don't we just meet again for lunch next week? You can finish your lecture on the appalling realities of publishing and also tell me what you think of *Home on the Road*.

M: All right. And I won't make any appointments that could cut us short next time. I'll take your manuscript home with me tonight, and by the time we meet next week I'll have a first reaction for you. But wait, there's something we haven't settled—the option clause. Who gets to choose the restaurant for this next lunch? I don't imagine you've been keeping yourself in exile out there in the country— you probably know the city better than I do. Anyway, let's take turns.

J: Fine. That's a good way to learn about new territories.

M: Are we up to it?

J: There's only one way to find out. For instance, I've been wanting to try a new Thai spot I just heard about.

M: Okay, I'm game. Now pass me the manuscript.

J: Michelle, just remember it's not your usual . . . maybe

I really ought to look into self-publishing for it, but . . .

M: Let me tell you what I think before you go cooking up any hare-brained alternatives. Who knows? Maybe you've got a potential blockbuster here.

J: Well, yes, I think it has great possibilities, but the idea of your rushing off with it to your office makes me feel so vulnerable. There are things I ought to explain . . .

M: No, I don't want to hear anything about it before I start reading. Just a clean slate. Relax, Jim! You're in good hands.

J: I know, but . . .

M: After all, how do you think I used to feel when you'd walk off into *your* office with an essay of mine? You'll live!

2

MENU TWO

Singha Beer
Thai Fish Cakes
Tofu Tod
(deep-fried tofu with vinaigrette sauce)
Mee Krob
(deep-fried bean thread noodles)
Squid Salad
Chicken Curry
Coconut Pudding
Banana Glacé

J: Hello! I'm glad to see you found the place. And in fine style too—what a great outfit! I could spend a whole day just watching you walk along the street.

M: These are my expedition clothes, special attire for this crummy neighborhood. But I've got to admit the restaurant has a certain charm—once you get over the bars on the windows and that Bangkok-blue paint.

J: And look at those tourist agency photos of the klongs. Don't you need a travel book written? We could spend a month over there and collaborate. Thailand looks like paradise.

M: Does paradise have proper food sanitation practices?

J: Come on, be adventurous. We wouldn't inspect the kitchens, just enjoy the eating.

M: Well, let's practice here first. I assume the food is going to be a pleasant surprise? We certainly won't be subjected to New York lunch prices!

J: One of my students says this place is supposed to have the best fish cakes this side of Surat Thani.

M: Know something weird? I just had the impulse to put up my hand and tell the class where Surat Thani is. What am I doing? You're not my professor anymore!

J: You look a little disappointed.

M: Because I actually *do* know about Surat Thani. One of my authors went to Thailand last year and ended up stuck there. It was too hot to do anything but stay in her hotel and eat, so she got addicted to some kind of shredded catfish. As for me, I'm adventurous enough to try anything once. In fact, at these prices I'll try *everything* once.

J: Michelle, when you were a student you were a kind and thoughtful soul. Has being an editor turned you into a sadist? Do you always make nervous authors sit through some idle chit-chat before you say what you think of their manuscripts?

M: Only authors who're thinking about self-publishing. No, I admit it, editors do engage authors in lengthy digressions. Maybe especially authors they like. We could talk quite a while about the character of editors, for instance. *Some* people realize what a fascinating topic it is.

J: Oh, it is indeed—especially yours, of course, but today my anxiety is overwhelming my gallantry, I'm afraid.

M: Sometimes we temporize because we can't bear to give someone we like bad news. Sometimes it's to soften up demanding authors before we tell them they have to cut their overweight manuscripts in half, or do a complete re-write. And sometimes it's just because there isn't any news, and they're going to have to wait for a decision.

J: Aha, now I can read that look! You haven't been able to get to *Home on the Road* yet, because there were thirteen manuscripts in line ahead of it. At least two of them had come in from big-gun agents who swore their commercial prospects were "awesome." Let's see, *The One-Minute Diet Book*, all about how you can lose a pound a day by setting a timer and only allowing yourself what you can cram down in sixty seconds per meal, and . . .

M: Are you giving that idea away? But more important, aren't you hungry? We can afford a lot more than sixty seconds.

J: Michelle, you're torturing me. I don't have the slightest appetite—I want to know what you think of my manuscript! Please!

M: Okay. I'll give out the grades before the lecture, and not hold out till afterward like one professor I used to know.

J: I quit that. The psychologists are right—rewards work much more effectively than punishments.

M: Well, you used to give rewards too—you once told me I was more fun to talk with than your colleagues. So you've trained me too well, you see. Conversation with you is like a wonderful long rally in tennis—how can you stand it when it ends? But enough, too much. I like your book, Jim.

J: You do? Really?

M: Your special voice comes through, strong and clear. I kept recognizing your rhythms, your intonations, but there are also new tones in it that I don't recognize yet. I didn't have the faintest idea what you meant by "America's Elders on Wheels" as a subtitle, but you grabbed my attention from the first page all right. It takes me into a world that I don't know anything about, and very convincingly. It's good clean writing and I'm sure it would be very informative to any retired person thinking of living that kind of mobile life. There are plenty of unusual sociological implications too—I can see where it must link up with your families book, because these people are forming new extended families for themselves, out there away from what we laughingly call civilization. But . . . I'm still not sure it's *publishable.*

J: If it's got all that going for it, why the hell not?

M: I'm going to play devil's advocate here, okay?

J: As far as I can tell, publishers are always devil's advocates.

M: Yes, and authors are the angelic host. So be angelic and listen. What I can't see is, who is the market for it, and how can we sell it to them? These old folks batting around out there on the highways don't sound like they spend a lot of time in bookstores—they're having too much fun with each other.

J: Wait a minute! This book isn't just for older people, it's about life in America in our times. The whole subtext critiques the way everybody else is tied into the fast-lane, high-consumption, stressed-out lifestyle of our beloved and accursed country. It's about vanishing American individuality. There are *still* unforgettable characters out there! And it poses some alternatives for simple, more satisfying ways to handle a lot of daily-life issues. What I'm trying . . .

M: I know that, Jim, and it's impressive, but as a publisher I have to think about the market, remember? Don't the people who are doing it already know how to lead the life?

J: There are always new recruits coming along! New people keep hearing about it and need to learn the ropes, and even the oldtimers *don't* have all the information. In fact, one of the main things they spend time on, when they circle the wagons out in some godforsaken spot, is precisely exchanging the kind of information I've collected in the back of the book—where the good camping places are, what different facilities are charging, cheap sources of food and equipment, how to take care of repairs while you're on the road, the latest thing in communications equipment, what to do about bikers, all that stuff.

M: Well, like I say, I found it fascinating. I guess I had thought retired people all lived in condos in Florida, like my grandparents, or maybe in "leisure communities." So it's certainly new material.

J: It's just not your idea of fun.

M: I didn't say that. I read it straight through like a shot, except for the appendix materials of course. The quality of the writing didn't surprise me, naturally. And it has a lot of curiosity value, but curiosity by itself isn't enough. What kind of reader have you been aiming at, in your own mind?

J: At God, basically. Don't laugh! I mean God as manifested in our dear friend, the General Reader. I really intend the book as a commentary on the current human condition. These elderly people have worked out a complicated and satisfying and rather bizarre life for themselves, on the fringes of society, living independently and pleasurably and supporting each other in their movable villages. It's strange and wonderful and I think a lot of readers would find it more than curious. It might even start some younger readers thinking about how *they* are using up their precious years. And what kind of urban environment they're living in.

M: So what you're really up to is trying to subvert the industrial way of life.

J: Exactly! Partly by conveying something of the beauty and strangeness of the empty parts of the country where these retired people feel most at home.

M: I thought that aspect of it was very good. It reminded me of Edward Abbey's attitude: humans have wrecked their cities and the suburbs are just cultural and social wastelands, so you have to learn to love the wilderness and find refuge there. But Abbey fans are mostly hiker types who want the wilderness to be left alone. Why will they care about elderly people in Winnebagos, for God's sake? They think Winnebagos are a heresy against Mother Earth.

J: So did I, until I finally admitted that I'd rather have a hot shower once in a while than live with a permanent accumulation of sweat. But the real point of the book is a social point, about the community these people have formed and maintained, about the old American dream of "heading out for the Territory." And making it there. Far from urban pleasures like Thai fish cakes. What do you think of them?

M: I have to admit it—they *are* the best I ever had. Thinner and crisper and well, just delicious. Are we going to try the tofu tod?

J: Only if I don't have to sing.

M: Not too bad. Did we ever make it to tri-lingual puns?

J: Once, I think.

M: I vote for linguistic simplicity and squid salad.

J: Don't forget the mee krob.

M: I'm sure I'll never forget it. But look, do you really think *Home on the Road* could sell in suburban chain stores?

J: Michelle, even suburbanites get older. Even suburbanites would like some freedom in their lives. Wait till they hear about the sexy parts.

M: That may be another problem. Do Americans want to read about grandparent types getting it on behind the sagebrush? Most Americans think aging is disgusting. They feel they're never going to get old.

J: That attitude's passing. We *are* getting older, the whole country. But that may not seem so bad if you realize that elderly people can still have very interesting sex lives. Some of these folks are as romantic as adolescents. No worries about pregnancy, and they don't pass diseases around. They can let their emotions run free. You read the part about what they call "multifidelity"?

M: Actually I thought that was a hippie concept.

J: Who knows? Maybe it was introduced out there by a former hippie, now aged sixty. Some trendy ideas don't die, they drift around and take root in odd places and flourish. I learned a lot about this country in those six months on the road. Most of what's really going on never makes it into the media. So this book is sort of a report from an unknown country—to its own inhabitants.

M: Well, to stop being so devilish, I've got to admit I

learned things from this manuscript. There's a lot of life in it, and it's sometimes delightfully funny. It does have a certain quirky appeal.

J: Then what do you think I should do with it? If you don't see a market for it, and nobody in New York wants it, perhaps it *is* something that self-publishing would be right for? I keep hearing that it's gotten much easier, and nobody worries about being accused of "vanity" publishing anymore. Too many good books have been self-published for that to stick. Successful books, too.

M: Yes, but . . . well, you've really done something novel, as far as I know. You aren't aware of any other books like it? Their track record might give some sense of whether there's an audience we could tap.

J: I *know* there aren't any. I researched it. Look, Michelle, I don't want to presume on our old feelings but . . .

M: Shut up a minute. Let's see . . . the last time my boss went along with a real wild card book was more than a year ago. I could be due for another one. I'm beginning to feel the book deserves a chance, Jim. Let me talk it over with him.

J: That's great, though I suspect his objections may be even more devilish than yours.

M: I'm beginning to see what's behind it for you. Maybe that should be brought out and discussed openly—make it a questioning of your whole former "normal" life. Then there could be more personal details. What it was really like around the campfires, with you the narrator searching the highways and byways for the lost soul of contemporary

America, figuring it must be out there somewhere, and then finding this unexpected vitality in the mobile elderly. Why, it could be a heroic quest story!

J: I thought I had enough of that in there, but there could be more, I suppose. —You know, looking back, you always had a tendency to see me as bigger than life size. It felt exciting as hell.

M: It's a good thing you didn't tell me that at the time. I thought I had to work hard to tempt you.

J: And all the while I thought you were tempting despite yourself, and I just lacked daring! —I used to wonder a lot what would have happened if I had just gotten you into bed one more time.

M: You're such a romantic, Jim. One more of anything never matters that much. Besides, if we *had* gotten together your colleagues would never have forgiven you. I've always assumed that was part of the story—you knew they wouldn't have invited you into their tenure club. You would have paid a heavy price.

J: Michelle, please believe me—the only thing I was conscious of at the time was the kids. I was too far gone to think about the tenure aspects. Or much of anything else.

M: Well, I'm not sure I would have wanted the responsibility anyway. You would've had to move on, live as an intellectual migrant laborer, or else change your line of work. Maybe even become a publisher!

J: But remember I don't have much business sense. At least your family had . . . what was it, a chicken farm?

M: How do you know that?

J: You told me one time when we were doing a poetry semester. You'd discovered that poetry tended to be an urban phenomenon, and it worried you to be a country girl. You seem to have gotten over that.

M: I probably overcompensated, by living in New York. But then editing can be a little like chicken-raising. You sometimes pick out a sort of runty one to be your favorite . . .

J: I hope that isn't what you're doing here! Look, I assume that if you thought *Home on the Road* was blindingly brilliant you would've been jumping up and down trying to sign me to a contract. My guess is that you're probably thinking it's not bad, it could be made better, but it would be a problem at Terra—which does some good books but isn't, when you come down to it, exactly a daredevil operation. In fact I would suspect there are only two really daring publishers of any consequence left, and one of them is probably on the verge of bankruptcy because its angel has just died and the other is about to be gobbled up by a conglomerate. The university presses are busy guarding their academic virginity. So anything truly innovative has to be done by little outfits, or self-published.

M: Jim, why so bitter? You're going to have to give me the whole story about your other books. Of course this manuscript doesn't make an easy situation for either of us. You're right, it *would* be a problem for Terra. I don't know how I could estimate the chances—why are you rolling your big blue eyes around like that?

J: Wait a minute. First I want to know whether I was right about your own personal opinion, factoring out all possible evil motives of revenging yourself upon my caddish behavior of yesteryear.

M: You're afraid I might reject it because you rejected me?

J: Something like that. Though I've always felt I didn't so much reject you as just bounce away, like some kind of pool ball—into the side pocket, where I've been ever since.

M: As far as I know, I'm rendering a detached professional judgment. I can't sit here and tell you it's blindingly brilliant, and I can't tell you it will sell. But in my considered opinion it's very well done, often surprisingly provocative, as they say. It's original. It has a wry quality of mind that's uniquely yours. It has important issues under the surface. It's a good book, and you can be proud of it.

J: Thanks. Thanks, old friend. Young friend. Whatever you are, thanks.

M: Oh, Jim, if you knew how hard it was for me to learn to tell any author . . .

J: I think I do know. It's like grading, remember. My feelings are so easily hurt, I assume everybody else's are too.

M: Well, they are. Except maybe for a few saints.

J: Here, you'd better take your hand back so we can get at that mee krob. It smells heavenly. I begin to have the distinct impression I'm going to end up as a self-publisher, but even so I really do want to hear the end of last week's lecture. I'm sure I'll learn something that a self-publisher would find useful.

M: And sordid. Not to mention ambiguous.

J: All right. We'd better get some more beer to go with this.

M: Yes, strengthen yourself, because I need to let you know more about what kind of thinking lies behind a decision to publish or reject. Keep in mind that if we should accept your book, we're agreeing to spend more than the down payment on a house. And you couldn't escape it either, just by saying "Whoopee, I'm a self-publisher." Let's see, how can I sketch out the Inside Picture. We could use a blackboard here, but I'll make do with these paper napkins. First come Editing Costs.

J: On *my* manuscript they'd be minimal, because it's polished to a gem-like finish. My word-processor is a more impeccable speller than the copy editors and proofreaders I've known.

M: But even the Gettysburg Address might have used a tiny bit of tidying up. And actually I spotted fifty or sixty things in your manuscript that your spelling program hadn't caught.

J: You *did?*

M: You know, "for" instead of "four" and so on—things the dumb machine won't notice. Missing words, superfluous hyphens, a few apparently missing lines . . .

J: I guess I should have given it a more careful last reading.

M: Yup. But don't feel bad—you'd be surprised how many authors can't spell, or punctuate, or keep grammatical parallelisms straight, or number footnotes accurately, or remember that they wrote the same thing in a previous chapter.

You'd also be surprised at how surly they can get when these shortcomings are pointed out to them.

J: I may grumble, but I do admit it when I'm wrong.

M: You do. I remember being surprised and delighted at that. None of my other professors could stand being caught out. Anyway, everything considered, it can cost well over a thousand dollars to edit a medium-sized serious book that's in as good initial shape as yours is—including the clean-up after it comes back from the author. Plus a couple of hundred for proofreading, and more again for indexing, if the author won't or can't do it. And you should see some of the jumbles that authors turn in as indexes.

J: Is your salary part of editing costs?

M: No, I'm an acquisitions editor. My mind is so scattered that no accountant could track the time I spend on different projects. So I count as Overhead. We'll get to that in a minute. Let's move on to manufacturing expenses. Authors don't like to hear such a crude term applied to their work. But it's useful to know how budgets divide up manufacturing costs. Plant Costs are typesetting, designers' fees, paste-up, proofs, negatives, printing plates, and in short everything up to the point where the book goes onto a printing press. Edition Costs cover paper, printing, binding, jacketing, and shipping books to the warehouse.

J: *Home on the Road* has no illustrations and I had a dream in the desert that it's going to sell a half million copies, so we can regard the plant costs as negligible. Besides, there are supposed to be miraculous reductions in typesetting costs because of new technology, lasers and all that. Leaving more money for Royalties.

M: I don't pretend to understand why, but new technology has a magical tendency to end up costing as much as old technology. At least when you add all the costs in and ask for truly comparable quality.

J: Another myth of progress, huh?

M: Maybe it's because the people who operate the new technology don't get any cheaper—they can even get more expensive, at least if they're good. You won't believe this, but one publisher found that hand-done calligraphy is actually cheaper than electronic typesetting. Anyway, the biggest cost in typesetting is paying a human being to hit the keys. And even though computers can now scan clean typescripts and set them in print, the only way to get editorial changes set cheaply is to persuade the author to do it free. Which is what self-publishers do, of course.

J: But if authors hit the keys for you, you *could* give them higher royalties. My manuscript is on diskettes, for instance.

M: Yes, and in editing it would get real messy. And if we did save anything, maybe we'd want to apply it to some of our losing books. A lot of bargaining goes on about royalty rates and advances, Jim. It's a tough business, in that area especially.

J: What's the average lately?

M: Royalties on reasonably salable hardcover books still hover around ten percent of the retail price, usually for the first five thousand copies sold, getting higher if more copies are sold. Advances go up and down like yo-yos, depending on whether publishers have been burned by making them too high lately. And depending on how much the authors need money.

J: I got ten percent and an advance of seventy-five hundred dollars for my *Families* book. Never saw another penny, either. But I know professors who get fifteen percent, on textbooks that are mostly regurgitation of other people's material.

M: There are established authors who get fifteen percent on formula novels. There are also many agents who get fifteen percent of what the author gets, instead of the old standard ten percent, thus leaving the author with twelve and three-quarters percent, minus expenses. Then there are authors who get fifteen percent but it turns out to be fifteen percent of the *net* receipts—that is, of the amount the publisher actually gets back from customers.

J: Hold it. Not a percentage of the price printed on the book?

M: No, "net" means what we get. Since bookstores receive discounts of at least forty percent on quantity orders, they pay to the publisher less than sixty percent of the retail price. In fact the publisher's net receipts these days may average down near fifty percent. So a net contract would make the author's royalty say fifteen percent times fifty percent, or about seven and a half percent of the retail price—*worse* than the author who is getting a straight ten percent on the retail price.

J: I think I get your nasty drift, and I'll bet a lot of authors don't realize this net business isn't just an innocent little distinction.

M: Well, authors are grown-ups—they ought to find out

about these things before they sign a contract. And protecting them is one of the things agents are for. You can do all right if you make sure you are getting your percentage of *all* receipts—some contracts cut off royalties altogether below a certain discount rate.

J: Jesus. You noble publishers wouldn't try to put something like that over on innocent authors, would you? Sounds like another way to drive us toward self-publication.

M: Actually net royalties are standard practice for textbooks, and for some university presses, and they're creeping into regular publishing too. But I've also known some greedy authors who deserved to get screwed, and did. Just keep in mind that royalties are always arrived at through negotiation. Negotiation is a matter of muscle, as one agent who used to be a philosopher put it, and I make no claims to moral perfection.

J: You've got good muscles, though. Not a comforting thought in this connection.

M: We'll see. Now onward to Advertising and Promotion. There used to be another rule of thumb that these expenses —including salaries, by the way—should roughly equal ten percent of what the publisher expected to take in on a book.

J: Typically backward publisher logic! Even I know that you have to spend money to make money.

M: But simply spending a vast amount of money won't automatically sell a vast amount of books. The real point is that the promotion budget is a finite amount. A dollar a copy is a standard some people use, so it isn't even a very large finite amount, for "middle books"—that is to say, the kind of books that most authors write: solid, useful, interesting books, but neither topical enough nor sleazy enough to sell millions or get made into movies.

J: You're talking about someone we know?

M: Sure. Your book is a classic middle book, and if you self-published it and spent twice what we would spend on advertising, I doubt if it would make a ten percent difference in sales. It isn't cost-effective, for a middle book, to plaster it all over the *New York Times Book Review* for six weeks. You'd have to sell thousands of extra copies to cover the cost, and it just wouldn't happen.

J: I don't like the idea of being stuck in that "middle book" category. It has the sound of a self-justifying hypothesis.

M: Yes, but editors are congenital optimists. We almost always start out thinking a book we've signed up is going to sell well. Still, on the average we end up with the same sort of percentage. Let's work it out for the bottom end of the feasibility scale: a $16.95 book sold directly through a bookstore brings the publisher, at the most, $16.95 times sixty percent or $10.17.

J: Not much.

M: So if you sold forty-five hundred copies entirely to bookstores, that would generate income of—umm, let's see—$45,765. But since maybe half of those copies would be sold through distributors, who get a better discount, or under other special conditions, the actual income would probably be something like $42,000. Ten percent of this for advertising and promotion is $4,200.

J: That still leaves $37,800—which can't all be spent on editing and printing. I'd want ads in the *New York Times* and about six major regional newspapers, the *New York Review of Books,* the *New Yorker,* and a few specialized publications.

M: And you might get some of them. Just be glad you're not being published by a really big house that does hundreds of books a season. A lot of their books don't get any promotion money *at all,* unless and until they begin to sell. But now let's finish up with our basic budget. The remaining major expense category is Overhead.

J: Why is it so enormous? That looks like a third more than everything you pay for printing and editing.

M: This is one category where a self-publisher *can* be more economical than a normal publishing house. Overhead means office rent, telephones, utilities, travel, supplies and postage. And my salary—and lunches. By the way, if you aren't going to eat the rest of that chicken curry, can I have it? It's terrific.

J: Sure. I notice you can eat and talk at the same time more gracefully than anybody I've ever seen.

M: Trick of the trade, like breathing for a singer. Are you up for dessert?

J: Who loves eating, loves life. Plunge from pleasure to pleasure. Those are quotes, I think, but my head is too full of numbers to remember from what. I'll get the coconut pudding and we can share.

M: Okay, I'll try this banana thing. Now back to sweet

overhead. It also has to cover the salaries of my bosses. Plus the salaries of the people who handle sales, production, accounting, warehousing, and invoicing. And collections.

J: What's "collections"?

M: Going after bad debts. You'd be surprised how hard it is to get money out of bookstores, not to mention small wholesalers with obscure addresses and bad payment records. These are all things that intrepid self-publishers forget they're going to have to spend time on, and won't get paid for. Anyway, what's left here at the bottom is Profit—or Loss, in which case you have to raise your price or get ready to swallow hard.

J: Why haven't you penciled in the profit figure? It looks like it should be . . . maybe $5,000?

M: Because it's probably a myth. On many books, more than half, you won't sell your projected forty-five hundred copies. So the losers have to be covered by the winners. We should really calculate the break-even point—how many copies we'd have to sell to cover our outlays. Actually, if there was too much reality in budgets, it wouldn't look good to the accountants. So you fall back on the handy rule that if you set your retail price at six or seven times your manufacturing costs, you should come out all right—if the book sells decently.

J: That's appalling! You know, I just heard from a computer-freak friend that self-publishing is getting really easy now, and this kind of thing makes me think I'd better look into it. I'd give away my books before I'd charge that kind of mark-up!

M: Well, that's an option a self-publisher is perfectly free to consider. If you're crazy enough.

J: Nobody who's a publisher has the right to call anybody else crazy.

M: But Jim, if you don't have any business sense it would be ridiculous to think of self-publishing. The manuscript is probably publishable, by a regular publisher. If it turns out Terra can't do it, you'll just have to find another one—somebody who has faith that there's a market for it.

J: And how am I supposed to bring off this small miracle? The manuscript has been rejected seven times so far. No, eight—I got another rejection the other day. Do you know how long it took me to find publishers for my other books? Two full years for the Faulkner study, and almost that for the *Families* book!

M: I can give you the names of a couple of agents. Even if we end up doing it, you should have an agent to handle the negotiations. No editor wants to fight directly with you about clauses 13 and 22. I think you can interest a good agent in this manuscript.

J: And one of these agents will tell me how he or she thinks my manuscript should be rewritten to be "more salable."

M: Sure. They're the go-betweens in this business.

J: Why do you look like you think that's good news? I'd bet you our lunch tab that they would tell me, for instance, to drop all that stuff about the legal rules of where and when and how you can sleep in a "house car." Which happens to be absolutely crucial for a mobile life.

M: You don't *have* to do what an agent suggests, and you can always change agents. Choose one who understands and likes the book and also can work for your interests better than you could yourself, especially your financial interests.

J: But I haven't found that wonderful agent yet. I tried getting an agent once. Two I approached said they couldn't take on new clients. After a bit, I got rejected by a couple of others, and three or four months had passed. The next agent, who was busier and more famous, took two months more, only to decide that he didn't think the manuscript could be sold because it was too long, probably because some nineteen-year-old reading assistant didn't finish reading it, and . . .

M: I'm sure glad I'm not nineteen anymore.

J: At nineteen *you* would have finished it! Anyway, for this reading, he didn't mind charging me money—which I take to be unethical, since an agent who gets income from fees on readings has no real incentive to *sell* manuscripts. So I can go through this process again and maybe finally some unknown agent will take it on—charging me an advance representation fee, fifteen percent on royalties, and passing on expenses for copying, postage, phones, telexes, lunches, messenger service, shoelaces, taxis, and tranquillizers— "without limitation," as it ominously says in one agent contract I've seen.

M: Glad you finally had to take a breath, so I can get a word in! Reputable agents don't charge reading fees. Though even bad news can be worth paying for, sometimes.

J: I don't need to pay anybody to learn that this manuscript is a problem for publishers. But damn it, Michelle, this is important stuff! The country *needs* this book. If it can only get out into the stores, there *is* an audience for it, I'm sure of that. It just doesn't fit into the usual categories. And agents and editors don't really like that—it obliges them to have to try to think. So their natural tendency is to say "Get rid of it!"

M: That's still no reason to give up on finding a publisher. Especially when you're having lunch with one who likes to think. As well as eat.

J: I didn't mean to insult you. But please don't lead me on. I'm considering self-publishing as a means of self-defense. I've been through several wars with publishers already, and I really just don't want to face it again.

M: You're right that I can't sit here and tell you that Terra will do your book. But surely you'll give me the chance to see what we could work out?

J: You might be able to convince me that Terra isn't quite as incompetent as most publishers, since at least it's smaller. But I seem to have become allergic to banging my head against walls. Of course I'm tantalized by the possibility that the two of us might be able to work together. But if this manuscript is such a problem child maybe there's a good case for just bypassing the whole process. And getting on with something else. I do have some ideas . . .

M: So you'd plunge in and try to do it all yourself.

J: I want to be a realist. For instance, I don't actually think the *New York Times* is going to review my book, no matter who publishes it. Among that sixty thousand books you were talking about, how many do they review each year, maybe a thousand? What with the faddishness of the process, they must miss at least half the really important titles. But a lot of those books seem to do all right anyway. Besides, if you'll forgive me, I'm thinking in a longer-term perspective. I like what Melville said—that he was writing the kind of books that "fail."

M: But is that what you really want, Jim? I think you're more like the guy in *Ride the High Country,* who says he wants to be *justified.*

J: Right before he gets shot, as I recall.

M: Yes. It made me cry. But I'm not ready to cry about you. Look, I promised you I would tell the truth, and I have. It's not a masterpiece, but it is an intriguing book and if I can convince myself it's financially feasible I'd be proud to publish it. I would in fact be delighted to publish it.

J: Whether it happened to be by your old professor or not?

M: Yes. Though that *is* an additional inducement.

J: Really?

M: Of course. Don't you realize you've been sitting here in my head all these years? You helped me learn how to think, and ever since then echoes of your way of thinking have kept going through my mind. So it would be a joy to work with you, to have the actual you in my real life again.

J: I may be more troublesome in real life than you think.

M: Probably, but you needn't look as if you expect a medal for it! Anyway, let me explain what's involved. In a bigger firm your manuscript would get a cold-eyed look by a bottom-line-oriented board of some kind—money people, sales people, subsidiary rights people. With Terra, the editorial side has more say, but it's still a cautious process. We meet once a week to discuss projects the editors bring in. I propose a book to the group, complete with budget, and they shoot at it from their different angles. If it survives that, and gets the boss's approval, then I can do it.

J: Well, that certainly gives me something to think about.

M: What, you mean you're not even going to let me consider it? Or at least mention it to my boss and see if there's a possibility?

J: I . . . well . . . I just don't know! Twice burned, and all that. I guess I need more feel of what Terra is really like— what I'd be in for if you did the book.

M: For Christ's sake, we're a decent smallish firm with quite a wholesome reputation. We pay standard royalties and give competitive advances. We have a good mix of fiction and nonfiction, and we're lucky to have a backlist with some big steady sellers on it—cash cows that help keep us solvent. So we're freer to be a little more innovative than firms in New York—that's why we can think of your book at all. We have a very good publicity operation and get a lot of copies into the stores. What more do you want to know, our Dun & Bradstreet rating?

J: Everything. Everything that would happen. How you and I would work together, for instance. How I could find out what's going on, or *not* going on. How we would resolve disputes about copy editing, production, publicity. How I could make sure this book wouldn't get abandoned after publication. Schedules. At least two more lunches' worth!

M: You know what editors are supposed to do with people like you? Besides sending you off to look for an agent? Tell you to take your damned manuscript and stuff it down the . . .

J: But you're not going to do that, are you?

M: No, I'm not. We're going to have another jolly lunch next week and I'll tell you why self-publishing could ruin your life.

J: I'd better do some more homework about it then. Actually, I bet you're beginning to enjoy having me around, so you can't get away with any bullshit about what a genteel profession publishing is.

M: I *would* miss you. For a lot of reasons.

J: You know, if you want the truth, I . . . well, can I ask if you're seriously involved with anybody?

M: Impertinent curiosity, professor! But since you ask— not at the moment. When I was in New York I lived with a man, a painter. He was very dashing. We had a loft and everything that goes with it. He was getting to be a big name, and we were into all that gallery political life: hard partying all the time, too much coke around, and everybody either on the make or desperately trying to enjoy what or who they'd made.

J: And one day you woke up and realized it was non-survival behavior.

M: Yeah—as the old cliche says, the going ups weren't worth the coming downs. So after a while I had to get out. Since I came here, mostly I've just been working and hanging around with some old friends, and nothing terribly important has happened romantically. Sometimes I think of *Hamlet*: "The readiness is all." But then I realize I'm not positive what I'd be ready for. I used to feel I should start to think about getting married. But I still don't know if I'm up for dealing with real children.

J: Books don't talk back.

M: Their authors do.

J: Not me. I'm almost pathologically nice.

M: You're an idealist with an over-protective sense of irony. But then I'm an idealist too. —Now that we don't have that academic taboo hanging over us, how about a friendly hug for the road?

J: You read my mind. We'll have to try and stand up without knocking over the beer bottles . . .

M: I got to thinking about mind-reading while I was reading your manuscript. There's a line from Christopher Morley about "mere" words, something like "What else comes from so deep inside?"

J: And you publishers manage not to forget that, even in the midst of all your budgeting and scheming?

M: Sometimes, with the right author.

J: Come here, then. Um, that feels good.

M: Yum. When we—I must have felt like I was scared stiff, literally.

J: I was a wreck myself. Anyway, now you feel all warm and relaxed.

M: I did two years of bioenergetics therapy to make friends with my body.

J: It must have worked. Just the kind of cuddly critter I'd be willing to trust with my manuscript. For one more week, anyway.

M: You're on.

MENU THREE

Domestic Beer
Spinach Salad with Sesame Dressing
Spanish Omelet with Salsa
Mushroom Omelet

J: You sure sound grumpy today, Michelle. Cheer up—come sit over here where you can get a look out the window. What a charming courtyard they have out there! How did you find this cozy little place? You do live a civilized life!

M: I've tried everything in the neighborhood, down to the last sandwich joint. This is one of my refuges.

J: Yes, you could make yourself right at home here, I can see. I don't know about this "Omelets for Every Taste" on the menu, but there must be something hearty that would fix you up. Do you want to tell me what's wrong?

M: I'm a little hung over. Went out dancing last night and overdid it, I'm afraid.

J: I thought you editors were all workaholics and spent every evening reading manuscripts—if you didn't stay late at the office filling out book budget forms.

M: Gimme a break, Jim. A hard-working woman has to have some fun.

J: Well, did you have, uh, fun? You look terrible.

M: Yeah, I went out with an old friend. Don't be nosy.

J: Sorry.

M: Come to that, what did *you* do last night? For all I know, you could be living with somebody and have two more kids.

J: I'm not living with anybody. I worked on lecture notes and watched *My Night at Maud's.*

M: Drooling over Maud.

J: Shows good taste, doesn't it?

M: Then I bet you stayed awake working on a list of authors' grievances about publishers, which you're going to annoy me with in my weakened condition. Why don't we talk about beauty, or justice—one of those big fat Great Ideas? You know a lot more about them than you do about publishing.

J: No quarter today, I see. You should have a Spanish omelet with plenty of salsa. That'll clear your head and put some bounce back in your step. I'll have a mushroom one. And we ought to have some of this spinach salad with the sesame dressing.

M: *You* have it. I'll have just a sip of that beer. Mmmm.

J: Yes, take it easy but *take* it, as Studs Terkel says. Here, I'll put the beer halfway between us, the way we used to do. And now tell me—what's the news from your boss?

M: When I told him about your manuscript and asked him if I had another wild card coming, he just smiled inscrutably and said he'd look over the sales printouts on my books and let me know. Didn't throw me out of his office, so I think we have a chance.

J: "We," huh? Well, if he gets around to saying something like yes or no . . . Meanwhile, meet the new desk-top self-publisher!

M: Oh, shit. Spare me.

J: I mean I'm happy you want to see if you can do anything with the manuscript, but I'm fighting the temptation to believe that Terra will actually decide to publish it. Sometimes I even wonder if the damned thing is raising obstacles in the way of our getting to know each other again.

M: Could be. Though I seem to remember it was the manuscript that brought us back into contact.

J: Maybe it's served its purpose, then. Anyway, I've done a pile of reading about self-publishing since last week, and I begin to see there are a lot of positive reasons to go the self-publishing route. I've also been hearing about people around here who've published their own stuff and done very well, thank you. Turns out that my dog's veterinarian sold twelve thousand copies of his book by direct mail. Another guy sold fifteen thousand copies of a novel and then peddled the mass-market rights to a New York house. Kept his own edition in print too, just in case theirs was put out of print—which it was, soon enough. In short, self- publishing isn't just a second-class alternative to regular publishing. Sure, I'm fed up with what publishers have done—and haven't done—with my other books. But what I see now is that self-publishing can be quicker, easier, and a whole lot more fun. And I might even make more money!

M: Well, of course there have been success stories in self-publishing. I'm even willing to admit that quite a few of those sixty thousand titles are self-published these days.

But Jim, how much do you know about the publishing process as a business? Remember the old saying: doctors who treat themselves have fools for patients. Just because you have a word processor and can get your type set doesn't mean you're going to be an effective publisher. I know you have an omnivorous mind, but I bet you don't know the difference between serifs and sarsaparilla. And you haven't got a glimmer about distribution and publicity.

J: A lot of publishing firms aren't effective publishers either. If they were, authors would never have had to figure out how to self-publish.

M: But don't forget the authors who self-publish and sell two hundred copies to friends by twisting their arms, and lose all their investment. With no publisher to blame for it, either! Besides, I'll bet you have no idea what those others went through to sell all those copies—and how little writing they got done while they were selling them. Do you really want to be a bookkeeper and accountant, and spend your time doing sales records and tax returns?

J: If I can manage my income tax, I'm sure I can handle it. I'll just do a little less gardening for a while, that's all. As far as the publicity side goes, even if I had a publisher I'd end up doing most of that anyway. Publishers don't have the time or energy for it, except on a couple of lead books each season.

M: Jim, I have great respect for you, but I have to say you're a pretty typical author. Just because you've had a little bad luck with publishers or heard stories from disgruntled authors . . .

J: I wouldn't call it bad luck, it's standard operating procedure. As for horror stories, I just heard a new one, about an author whose name was misspelled on the jacket. It was supposed to be Rigg, but three thousand copies were in the stores before anybody realized it was printed as Pigg . . .

M: Don't waste my time with hearsay. There's nothing more vicious than author gossip. Talk about creative writing! Let's stick to your own personal experiences. The truth, remember?

J: God, where to start? Maybe at the end? Okay, I spend four years of my life writing *Families,* which I would immodestly consider a high-middle book. After two years of assorted traumas we can come back to later, it's duly published, or perhaps we should say "released." The sales reps are too busy selling cat books and movie-star autobiographies to pay much attention. They end up selling four thousand of the ten thousand copies that were printed.

M: Plenty of decent books sell worse.

J: And when it begins to get serious reviews—good ones, with the exception of a few idiots—by then it has vanished from the bookstores. A year or so later I learn it's out of print, just when professors get around to assigning it in courses.

M: You're not alone. Ninety percent of trade books are gone inside eleven months. And on the average one out of three copies are returned to the publishers unsold.

J: Well, if my experience is good luck, I hate to think what bad luck would be! Mind you, nobody *tells* me the book is out of print. I only discover it through a royalty statement, which is deliberately contrived to be unintelligible to anybody except an accountant. I am outraged, but I heroically control myself and call to ask what happened to the other six thousand copies, and why hadn't I heard anything about this decision? My editor doesn't know— that's not his department, nobody told *him* anything.

M: Hey, I had forgotten you had a talent for raving like that! It's beginning to bring my appetite back. I can actually taste the salsa.

J: They make a good omelet, all right. There's even a proper trace of onion in with the mushrooms on mine. Want a taste?

M: No, thanks, just go on—what happened? The books got shredded?

J: Yes, so I can't even buy some, as my contract says I could. They're gone, and nobody thought to offer any of them to me. Thus passing up some income, by the way— publishers are really so inept they're suicidal! So libraries can't order them, and I can't even get a couple of hundred to sell over the years, at lectures or to friends and relatives or through the Buckley-Little Catalog. Can I sue? Well, I looked into it, and found that the National Writers Union had sued for Alvah Bessie, and actually got his publisher to agree to print up replacement copies. It took a couple of years, and the agreement came through the day after he died.

M: Bring on the violins.

J: Bring on the whole *Requiem*—this stuff happens all the time! One guy I heard of was lucky enough to get a mass-market paperback edition. He wondered why he never saw it on the racks and then one day he phoned the publisher to buy fifty copies and discovered it was out of print—the publisher had pulped all eighty thousand copies! Then there was the author whose publisher lost her books when they switched warehouses—just physically lost them, for five months. Not to mention the publishers who mistakenly tell would-be customers that a book is out of print when they still have thousands of copies lying in the warehouse.

M: Well, we always know where every last carton of books is, and how much dust is on it.

J: Okay, but I hope Terra isn't among the publishers who start to remainder books practically before they hit the stores. When I had a heart-to-heart chat with my local friendly bookstore owner about why he no longer had *Families* in stock, he told me the average shelf-life of a new book in the chains is something like six weeks. So he felt proud that he had kept it in stock for six months.

M: His pride was justified. If you look at the numbers, a book has to sell about seven copies a year in any given bookstore or it doesn't pay for its own shelf space. When sales drop lower than that, some new title takes its place. Do you think your book deserved charity or something?

J: Books are the intellectual life's blood of this country. Nobody's asking for anything more than decent treatment for them.

M: Sure you are. Face it, Jim, bookstores have to pay at least as much attention to their leases as to books, or they wouldn't be there next week.

J: Well, some of them barely pay attention to books at all. A lot of clerks won't even look up a title in *Books in Print* because it's easier to use the limited list on a distributor's microfiche—and besides, the customer might decide to *order* a copy, which means somebody would have to do the paperwork. And the buyers! I've talked to one or two of them, and the riskiest thing they ever do is drive to the store.

M: And both publishers and authors are utterly dependent on them. But remember there *are* some wonderful independent bookstores. Their staffs love books and know their trade and are somehow willing to work at miserable wages. They're our real friends.

J: When you sigh like that you break my heart. But what I've learned is that the whole bookstore blockade is being by-passed by a lot of hot-shot self-publishers who sell most of their books through the mail.

M: Yes, sure. But what if I don't have an overwhelming passion for how-to books, which are what sell best through the mail? What if my real delight is publishing fiction and ecology and political stuff—books that prospective readers want to browse in before they buy? You think it's *fun* to go into a bookstore that features almost nothing but romance novels and pop-psych and get-rich-quick books?

J: At least the stores might have the grace to wait till the reviews come in before they turn their computer loose with its bloody hatchet.

M: Hey, you got off a pretty good sigh there, too! But a lot of independent bookstores keep books in stock a long time.

J: All fifty-nine of them.

M: Nonsense, there are at least sixty. Or two hundred. Anyway, you won't get much argument from me about publishers screwing up on closing books out. Though it's usually just overworked and overhassled people trying to do the best they can. Our main responsibility is to the new books coming along.

J: Yes, authors can be held to high standards of performance, but publishers are allowed to be incompetent because they're busy!

M: Or hung over. Give me another sip of that, and come on, Jim, *you* take it easy.

J: Nope, authors can't afford to be merciful if publishers are going to be merciless. Just before I came in, I was reading some handy hints about book design for self-publishers, and that reminds me of all the heartburn authors get from how publishers handle design. Why don't they hire some first-class designers and develop truly lovely and readable standard designs, the way the British did with the Penguin series?

M: Some of us would love to do just that. But Americans are allergic to standardization. We won't even accept the metric system.

J: Bull. We standardize everything, down to the percentage of fat in a fast-food hamburger. You just have to conceal the standardization—behind dramatically different dust-jackets, for instance. But there are a lot of other things that get concealed that ought not to be. I've heard of publishers editing a manuscript and then having it typeset without even showing the author what they've done to it.

M: Don't push me too far, Jim. I'm not my fellow publishers' keeper. Besides, if you saw the garbage that some authors can produce, you might wonder about the point of letting them look at the improvements a good editor wasted her precious time making. They wouldn't appreciate it and they certainly couldn't do any better!

J: I'm not trying to be unpleasant. I just want to suggest why a lot of authors are beginning to make end runs around you publishers. I'm telling you what your best author friends won't tell you.

M: Oh yes, they will! They already have. I see I've got to switch from defense to offense here. Like what would you as a self-publisher do about distribution? Are you expecting bookstore buyers to beat a path to your door? How are you as a one-book publisher without any leverage going to collect money from non-paying stores?

J: Well, I'll try to get some of the regional distributors that are sympathetic to small presses to handle it for store sales. Then I'll have to rely on direct mail and small ads in publications that reach older people. Did you know that the American Association of Retired Persons has about ten million members?

M: Sure it does, and to reach them with a flyer would cost you three or four years' salary. And you might or might not get enough orders to pay for the mailing and the books.

J: Yes, but the self-publishing manuals explain how to test the waters with a small sample mailing. Then if that makes money it would be rational to spend more on a bigger mailing.

M: Okay, that might work. But do you think you'll get the book into stores by sending out flyers to bookstore buyers, who only give official sales reps about fifteen minutes to sell their entire line?

J: Actually I'm not too discouraged about bookstores. In fact, I think older people buy quite a lot of books, and I'd just do a small mailing to a couple of hundred good stores. I figure that if I can get one or two wholesalers to handle my book, that would give me enough of a start to know if the thing will sell. I'm not shy, you remember, so I'm also not afraid of calling on bookstore buyers and pleading my case. Besides, I have some wonderful publicity ideas up my sleeve.

M: You're going to have a book signing party in Monument Valley? Forgive me, Jim, but back up, please. Manuscripts need editing, you know. On a first reading, I don't think this one needs major reshaping, but it certainly could use an editor's serious help. I was mentioning some things that could use filling out, and there are plenty of places that could be polished, tightened, and . . .

J: I have in mind to hire a freelance editor. An underemployed former aspiring novelist friend who can also proofread.

M: You'll get what you pay for—just the minimum necessities, and maybe not even that.

J: Considering the quality of editing I got on those other books, the publishers didn't get what they paid for either.

M: All right, if you're so smart, how are *you* going to manage design and typesetting and layout?

J: The manuscript is on diskettes. I can page it on my computer, just copying the design of an existing book that I like. Then I'll have it spat out at a copy service, or borrow a laser printer from somebody at the college. I'm compulsive enough to prepare the camera-ready copy—there are books about doing it, mostly self-published. Then I'll get bids from three short-run printers in the Midwest and do about twenty-five hundred copies, case-binding and jacketing five hundred for reviewers and libraries. It won't win any prizes for design or typography, but neither do most books. It'll be perfectly readable. I could even do without ligatures and kerning—a self-publisher named Walt Whitman did, I believe.

M: Jim, you've been holding back on me! Where did you learn all that insider vocabulary?

J: I did a lot of homework this past week. From what I've been reading, the distinction between publishing insiders and outsiders is rapidly diminishing. As far as I can see, before long it'll be electronic publishing of some kind for most specialized books. The manuscripts will be written on computers, and stored in central computers, or on laser discs you can send through the mail and store in some kind of juke-box contraption, and people will stick in their credit card and print books out only if and when they want to have a copy. What will we need publishers for then?

M: God, you go for the jugular, don't you? Give me that beer! Well, all right: somebody will have to screen out the junk so that the system doesn't get even more overloaded than it is with printed books. Also, I suspect that an electronic publishing system might work fine for an academic study of Faulkner's late style, which would only be wanted by maybe three hundred colleagues and a couple of handfuls of university and college libraries, but it isn't going to work for general-interest books, even for a lot of middle books, or for fiction.

J: At least you didn't say "a pedantic study" of Faulkner.

M: Come on, I'll bet what you think about Faulkner is extremely interesting. And I intend to catch up on what you said about families too—though I sure as hell wouldn't want to read it in some floppy, faded printout.

J: You're just trying to get on my good side. But I'm beginning to be convinced that *Home on the Road* may not be easy to sell. So okay, if I don't like the frying pan and I don't fancy the fire, what am I supposed to do?

M: Well, you might let me have a week or two more, before you give up on publishers forever.

J: I suppose so, but I'm just not cut out for martyrdom. Can't you see what a relief it would be to pass the manuscript on to my copy editor and stop worrying?

M: You can stand a week or two of suspense! Consider the real alternative: to publish *Home on the Road* yourself will cost you hundreds and hundreds of hours of work, not to mention risking at least five grand, even on an austerity budget. Can you spare it?

J: No, but easier than I could spare another year and a half of pissing around, hoping and waiting for the book to get out. Some of the work of putting it together would actually be fun, sort of like home carpentry. And I have a couple of friends who are probably willing to put a little money into it if I need it.

M: Those must be real friends! And you may still be the most remarkable person I've ever met, because it has just dawned on me that this is an extremely odd situation. Ordinarily authors are pleading with me to publish their books, even if it takes years, which it sometimes does. Your manuscript has been growing on me, and I'm willing to take a run with it in our shop. Yet you're dragging your feet. What's going on here? Are you pre-emptively rejecting me and Terra Books out of a fear of being rejected yourself?

J: I don't think so. It's just that authors are in such a weak position in this business that we need to be super-humanly careful.

M: Look, I can't take any more of this—let's get out of here. I need to walk around for a while and just breathe.

J: You're really in bad shape, aren't you? Poor sweetie. Come on, then—it's actually a lovely day outside. Very breathable.

M: We'll see about that.

J: There you are—patches of blue sky, gentle breeze. We can stroll down toward the water for a while. Here, take my arm. Hang on. Step, breathe, step, breathe.

M: I think I'm going to make it. If you feel me suddenly veering toward the gutter, it'll be either because I'm going to throw up or because I see an author coming.

J: Somebody like me, probably, wanting to complain about a copy editor trying to obliterate what you were kind enough to call my distinctive voice. You know, I finally had to threaten to sue my *Families* publisher for damage to my professional reputation. Then they called off the first copy editor, went back to a clean manuscript, and started over—once over lightly. When the book finally came out, the reviews all praised my sprightly style.

M: So you see, publishers can be flexible and responsive. And at least semi-intelligent. Jim, look, you *know* me. You saw a lot of me for three whole years. Am I a raving irresponsible maniac? Why don't you think I'd treat you and your book decently?

J: It's not you, it's the *institution* I'm talking about. I just don't believe you can really control it. Probably your boss can't even control it. But as a self-publisher I'm sure I can control myself. That would be worth a lot in peace of mind. Take inscrutable delays. My Faulkner manuscript was handled by perfectly decent people, but it sat on a lot of desks for incredibly long times. First it had to get checked to make sure it was ready to be okayed by a faculty overseeing committee . . .

M: That was to make sure you didn't disgrace the university. University presses don't trust mere editors to decide things like that. With us, acceptance is a lot simpler and quicker, believe me.

J: Then it sat waiting to be assigned to a copy editor. And then it sat on a designer's desk for a while, and then it got to sit on a production person's desk. Finally it went off to the typesetter, and then came back in proofs and sat on somebody else's desk to ripen for a while, and finally got ready to go on the press. If I had been self-publishing that one, I could have had it ready to print by the time it moved from Desk A to Desk B.

M: It might have had footnotes mixed up, or wrong running-heads, or whole paragraphs omitted, or . . .

J: Then again, it probably would have looked perfectly all right. I do have a compulsive side. I *like* details. I like them even better when they're handled right. Shall I show you the errata slip I worked up?

M: No, no, no! We have very good proofreading. Though I still remember an antique inscription that a wily old editor friend in New York had on his office door: "There is No Booke but in which Error has affixed his Sly Imprimatur."

J: I bet that meant doctrinal deviation. Some medieval priest was out to burn people and their books, and that was his slogan.

M: Cool off. We're just after typos.

J: Okay, then comes more trouble. The book gets printed, the poor sap of an author thinks the whole long trail of tears has been worth it. He's waiting for the bouquets from his many admirers. But it turns out that some copies had bunches of pages reversed or omitted in the bindery, or some have spotty areas so faintly printed that they can hardly be read, and by the time bookstores have discovered this and returned them for replacement copies, the publicity campaign is over. And so the books get returned for good this time.

M: Look, Jim, I can't even tell anymore if that's your story, or somebody else's story, or just some exaggeration you've cooked up. I've been trudging along listening to your bill of complaints and I am *tired* of all this. You must know

that quite a lot of books get published smoothly and success-
fully. I'm sure publishers do make a lot of mistakes. I know
I make some—but I'm also positive that if you try publishing yourself you'll make a few too. You've got to consider
the over-all picture. After all, the situation is no better in
other American industries. You want colossal mismanage-
ment? Look at the auto industry. Look at the banks, flinging
money down elephant-sized ratholes. And then, as I recall,
things are not exactly shipshape in academia, either, right?

J: You've got me fair and square, even if I've never been a
dean and never hope to be one.

M: Besides, wait till I catch *you* hung over and tell you
some stories about the abominations that authors can be
guilty of. Take the ones who sell the same book project to
two publishers, the ones who never deliver their manuscripts, the ones who plagiarize, the ones who commit libel
without warning anybody about it, the ones who can't
write a civil letter, or turn up dead drunk for television
shows, the ones whose delusions of grandeur make them
intolerable to a publisher's whole staff. But anyway, what
conclusion do you draw from all this—aside from the obvious fact that this is not the best of all possible worlds?

J: It's not the worst of all possible worlds either. I suppose
it's just the comedy of survival, isn't it? I admit that authors
do get books published, and some of them probably sell
as many copies as they deserve to. See how equable I can
be? In fact I actually feel much better, having that all off
my chest!

M: I wish I could say the same. But even conceding your
points, you'd *still* be better off if you didn't try to publish

Home on the Road yourself. You'd probably end up not
selling half the copies we could sell for you—even if we
didn't sell as many as you *thought* we should have.

J: Actually, half the copies at a quarter the heartache would
be a great publishing deal compared to my past experiences.

M: Jim, please . . . I'm getting attached to this brainchild
of yours. And I promise you that I can make publication
go well for you this time.

J: So you say, and I believe you believe it. But—Michelle,
I've been thinking hard, and on balance I just don't want
to risk it. No, you'd better give me the manuscript back.

M: What? Look, if we turn it down, you can go and self-
publish it just as you've planned! You're being totally impossible. What have you got to lose?

J: My pride, my sanity, my sacred honor, who knows how
many weeks or months of my time. Perhaps even worse.

M: Why the tragic look? How could there possibly be worse?

J: We could jeopardize our new friendship, you and I. We
find each other again after all these years, then we mess it
up. Boss rejects book, you feel guilty, I feel angry, we both
feel confused and resentful. Presto, no more lunches, no . . .

M: Now wait a minute. I seem to remember your being a
philosopher. Are you saying that in your values hierarchy
our uh, lunches rate as more important than getting Terra
to publish your book?

J: When I really stop to think about it, that's right.

M: I'm—well, our relationship is very important to me too. But you're just imagining trouble where there isn't going to be any. Jim, taking the manuscript back now would be a serious mistake. Don't hamstring an editor who's trying to help you!

J: Do I get my ribbon copy back at lunch next week?

M: What? You want me to give up on your book but sit down for another lunch, as if nothing's changed? What do you think I am?

J: I think you're a competitive editor who can't stand the thought of a book getting away, even a problematic one. And you're also the most wonderful woman I know. That's the whole point. And you can always keep on giving me advice. God knows I need it. Now draw yourself up to your full elegant height for a hug.

M: I don't believe this. *Publishers* reject *authors*, authors don't reject publishers. And then expect the publisher to . . .

J: Let's break another taboo, then.

M: One was enough, thanks.

J: But we'll meet next week?

M: I'll think about it. After all, I may have a hotter prospect. Or at least one who's sane!

4

MENU FOUR

White Wine

Garden Vegetables:
Tomato, Cucumber, Pepper, Pea Pods

Sandwiches

Potato Chips

J: Aha, there you are, Michelle. I'd begun to think you were still so mad at me that you'd decided not to come. Or else that I'd mixed up the date. I *was* really terrible to you last week, I know. My apologies.

M: So that's why you were pacing back and forth. No, I've gotten over last week and I've been itching to see you. It must be some kind of perversion! I just got held up—had to talk with our production manager about getting a book back on schedule.

J: A laggard author hadn't returned proofs on time?

M: How did you guess? Now people have to work overtime to get the book out—a big chainstore order could be canceled if we don't have copies available as promised.

J: Well, you're here and we're still speaking to each other. All my anxieties are allayed. Come on, let's walk up through the park to that hill.

M: Yes, a little exercise before our picnic. Being an editor sure is hard on the body.

J: So's writing, remember? But I've brought some good healthy stuff from my garden. Tomatoes, cucumbers, peppers, pea pods.

M: I've brought sandwiches.

J: I've got the wine.

M: And I've got the potato chips. But what's *that*?

J: An artichoke flower corsage for you. I'm experimenting with edible landscaping. This is too far along to eat, of course. You can dry it out—it'll keep.

M: Purple's my favorite color. Looks good against my jacket, doesn't it? How soft the top fringes are. Not sure about these spines though. Yi!

J: They're sharp, all right. An interesting combination?

M: I like it. It's beautiful, but looks as if it could hold its own in the wild. Maybe the same principle as that denim jeans and fancy shirt combination. Your carefree country-gentleman outfit.

J: I wanted to impress you.

M: Well, you always impress me. What else do you grow out there?

J: Scarlet runner beans. Asparagus. Rhubarb and grapes. You know I've always had fantasies of self-sufficiency. That's what really appeals to me about living in the country.

M: What I like about the country is the opportunity for long poetic walks. —Why are you looking at me like that?

J: I've finally figured it out—you *move* differently than you used to.

M: How so? I thought I was just putting one foot in front of the other.

J: I'm not sure exactly. It's as if you're more at home in your body. The way a cat is. It's beautiful to see.

M: Well, thanks! —Does that look like a proper picnic tree over there?

J: Definitely a literary tree—reminds me of *Ferdinand the Bull.*

M: Maybe it'll keep the rain off if those clouds come our way.

J: That's a stylish picnic hamper you've got. I assume my manuscript is in there next to the sandwiches, ready to return to me?

M: Jim, let's not get back into your fantasies about self-publishing. There's a new development at Terra. My boss has decided I *do* have a wild card coming. When I told him your manuscript has Literary Merit he warmed up to it. And he also said we've got to recognize that the book-reading audience is getting older. Maybe your book is the first sign of a new trend! So I've made some copies to do a little market research, asking people "Would you buy this book?" I gave one to a just-retired engineer I know, for instance. And I also sent one to a gerontology expert, to see what she would think of it.

J: I don't believe it. It's *my* manuscript, for Christ's sake! How can you do market research on it if I'm not sub-mitting it?

M: I've kidnapped it. It's growing on me, as I said.

J: It is? I'll be damned!

M: I reread some parts of it and—you know, I still don't think it has great sales prospects, but it's so well observed and so witty that I think we ought to go with it. Maybe it could be turned into some kind of offbeat hit. Unknown Americans and all that.

J: Really? But what does your boss think of my prose?

M: Oh, he hasn't found time to look at it yet. He promises he will this week, though, before he goes to New York for the sales meeting.

J: Did you explain the problems to him?

M: Of course. I told him you were headstrong, edgy, morose . . .

J: Handsome, urbane . . .

M: A superb speller, and a born troublemaker.

J: And he said?

M: He said that if you'd been my favorite professor you couldn't be all bad, even if you *were* an author.

J: Sounds like an okay boss.

M: He also reminded me that my last wild-card book lost the company twenty thousand dollars.

J: Wait a minute. How can a publisher lose twenty thousand on one book when a self-publisher only needs five thousand to put it out?

M: Oh, come on, we're talking about a professional operation where people get paid for doing things. Self-publishers who don't pay themselves for what paid employees usually do are committing auto-philanthropy. They're subsidizing themselves, eating their own overhead—a disgusting dish.

J: Unless you had no other choice.

M: You said it. Whereas a realistic budget provides for a decent print run, overhead, advertising, promotion, warehousing, billing, collecting, bad debts. —Maybe we should have had a surprise quiz. I'm not sure you're in shape for the mid-term.

J: Okay, I'll review my notes. But today, unless you want me to burglarize your office to get my manuscript back, you'd better come clean with just what I'd be in for if lightning strikes and your boss gives the green light on my manuscript and I, in a moment of temporary madness, accept.—Hey, do I feel a drop? Let me grab that sandwich.

M: You want all the grubby details?

J: Every one.

M: Let's put a few things back in the hamper, just in case. But give me another tomato—they're delicious! First, of course, we'd negotiate a contract, agent or no agent. We'd offer you a modest sort of package—probably ten percent on clothbound copies, seven percent on paperbacks, going up to eight after maybe ten thousand copies were sold. We'd give you only a small advance, maybe five thousand dollars.

J: That doesn't sound like something to make dollar signs start flashing in an agent's eyeballs. Do you figure you have me over a barrel since the book is already written? If I wrote you a prospectus and pretended I was just starting on it, would you give me a decent advance? To cover my travel expenses at least?

M: No, it's just not a conventionally competitive book—unless you get over your distrust of agents and find one who can interest other publishers in it too. Then we'd be bidding against each other, and that can make the competitive juices flow. But Terra still wouldn't go very high. One thing about not being in New York, we don't get caught in those bidding fevers that can run advances up to three or four times what a book's likely to earn back in royalties on sales. And about travel expenses, I thought you had gone on vacation to restore your soul.

J: You're certainly making make me feel wanted. Is this studied faint interest a standard negotiating ploy? Look, we'd better rearrange this stuff and pull the end of the blanket up over our heads to keep the drizzle off.

M: Great idea. Got enough room? You can move closer, you know.

J: Even if you *are* a publisher? How's that? How about maybe even an arm around?

M: Feels fine! Look how lovely those trees are over there, in the mist.

J: Maybe we'll just have to sit here for the whole afternoon.

M: Then hand me my wine glass, will you? Now where were we? Do we care? Oh, yes. Some other editor might disparage your book to beat you down on terms, but I'm still just faithfully carrying out my promise to tell you how publishers think, remember?

J: I believe you, especially since your hair smells so good when it's damp.

M: You'd better, or I'll take my blanket and go home. Anyway, you could get us to sweeten a few of the minor terms, but the basic deal is pretty set by the nature of the book.

J: So no matter how many lunches we had, or how I raged and screamed and called you a robber, I'd never convince you this might be a best seller, something like another *Zen and the Art of Motorcycle Maintenance.*

M: But the point is that the deal would be fair under the circumstances, which is all you can ever go by. Since it's not a flat-fee purchase but a deal based on royalties, you'll do well even if the book only sells half of what you think it should. Not to mention the outside possibility that it turns out to be an everlasting classic.

J: I'd be protected against success.

M: You might put it that way, if that perspective really makes you feel good.

J: I'm already feeling good, snuggled up with you here.

M: Well, so am I. And I love that great boyish grin on your face! You haven't looked that happy since—well, a long time ago.

J: Michelle . . .

M: No, one arm's enough for now, Jim. We've got to be very careful with each other this time, please. And this is still a publisher's lunch, remember.

J: Well, okay. Back to business—reluctantly! It *did* occur to me that since you wouldn't have much advance money laid out, you'd also be protected against having to work really hard to try and get it back. One author friend told me, "Look, honey, the money you see up front is all you're going to get."

M: You're mixing up issues there. You're right that we'd be keeping our initial financial exposure limited. If you were in my place, or just devising your own best strategies as a self-publisher, you'd do the same thing, because that's the nature of the situation. You're not going to sell your house and furniture and print fifty thousand copies of *Home on the Road,* even if it pushed the price down to $11.95. But royalties are another question. I can show you pay sheets for plenty of our authors who've been getting checks for years. Do you think we're thieves?

J: Let's just say that authors report some pretty strange phenomena in royalty accounting forms. Like mysteriously rounded numbers and uncheckable returns figures. And from what I hear, agents don't police royalty statements unless huge amounts are involved. They tend to forget about a book once they've pocketed their percentage of its advance. So I want it in my contract that I can walk in the door any time and look at the raw sales printouts.

M: You may not believe it, but we wouldn't have any objection to that. As long as you promise to be on good behavior while you're on the premises. Anyway, let's assume we've signed the contract and we're still speaking to each other.

J: How could two people who carried out a contract negotiation under a blanket stop speaking to each other?

M: Is *that* what we're doing?

J: I don't care what you call it, I like it.

M: Me too, but we can't get swept away.

J: No, there's other contract stuff to settle. I do think this has movie or TV possibilities, and since you're being so chintzy on the advance I think I should get ninety percent of that income, if there is any. There might be board games. Or dolls! I can think like a business person too, right? Stop that giggling!

M: You're ridiculous when you try to be a business person.

J: Who cares? Onward, ever onward! For instance, I want to clarify the process of giving the rights back to me if and when the book goes out of print. I'd want to define out-of-print in terms of a minimum number of copies sold in six months, rather than some vague "availability" phrase. That way if you're not selling it anymore you can't prevent me from reprinting it, or selling the paperback rights to somebody else, or licensing a translation or a movie, by procrastinating and claiming the book isn't really out of print—even though there haven't been any for sale for six or eight months, or eighteen.

M: Where did you get all these ideas? A reversion of rights to the author has to go through our legal department, to make sure the contract doesn't pose any unusual problems.

J: That's just hoping another turnip will come along to squeeze. So you can send it through the legal department three times if you feel like it, but if it's only sold twelve copies in the last royalty period and I send you a registered letter, the rights automatically revert to me, without any written acknowledgement being necessary. And that really is *not* negotiable.

M: God, you're getting tough! I've been teaching you too well. But I think that can be done. I'm making careful mental notes of all this.

J: You're one of the world's most endearing optimists.

M: Why shouldn't I be? We're working out the world's most innovative book contract, one that will make the world's most demanding author happy. Anything else you can think of?

J: If there's a movie deal signed, I want another and bigger advance. I want twenty-five free copies. And in case it's a smash, I want the income dribbled out, since I can't do income-averaging on my taxes anymore. Actually, I guess that's it, if I can reserve the right to think of some more later.

M: That's cheating, you know.—It looks like the drizzle's stopping.

J: Yes, but don't move or anything. It might sprinkle some more.

M: No, no, of course I won't. We have to go on with what would happen, once I had you securely signed up.

J: You're pretty good at maintaining suspense. Maybe *you* should be an author.

M: No. I wouldn't be any better at it than you'd be as a publisher.

J: Bumblers all!

M: Just shut up and listen, will you? Here, have a little more wine. Once the contract was signed and your royalty advance was in your bank, you and I would work on revisions to the manuscript. We'd be working soberly over a big table, not over lunch. Hard, careful work. I'd propose quite a lot of modifications and improvements. Partly small things, others rather large. I have a problem with your title, for instance. *Home on the Road* just doesn't do it for me. I can see the allusion you want to make to the song, but it makes it sound nostalgic, whereas your point is that something new is going on. Even with the subtitle and some kind of jacket tag line, it would . . .

J: All right, we could argue about that. I *like* arguing with you. But when it comes right down to it, who would decide?

M: You're doing either/or logic, Jim. Try some both/and. We both work on it and we find something we both like. It's your book. But it's our money. It's a partnership, not a courtroom trial. We're aiming at a marriage of true minds. Both people deserve to be satisfied.

J: You mean that, don't you? Fair-minded Michelle! But as a freebooter self-publisher, I could call it *Sex after Seventy in the National Forests* if I felt like it, and nobody could say me nay.

M: Why worry so much about nays? Working with an editor, you should be able to find the *best* title. Why are you so reluctant to consider accepting help? Does it make you feel you're losing control? I don't want you to feel I'm some kind of threat!

J: I'm being difficult again?

M: Right. It isn't becoming for you to carry on like that.

J: Learn to trust a little?

M: You said it! Anyway, after I'd done what I could on grand strategy, the manuscript would move on to a copy editor, who would subject it the closest scrutiny it would ever get from anybody, including you.

J: I know—paring down my stylistic flourishes, blindly following some editing manual's rules . . .

M: We'd be careful of your battle scars. We'd give you sample edited pages to look over, and if there was some kind of systematic mismatch we'd move you to another copy editor.

J: You would? I like that! But suppose we end up disagreeing about things? I can imagine being able to come to agreeable solutions for everything you and I would work on, but in three hundred pages of manuscript there are bound to be a lot of unresolvable differences with a copy editor.

M: It's your book, Jim. Once it's accepted, unless you ask to do something that's illegal or simply and starkly wrong, it would come out the way you wanted it. We might give you very stern advice, maybe even scream at you about it, but you would not be bound to accept it.

J: That's reassuring. I've spent two years of my life on this thing, you know, and I have a strong desire to get it printed the way I've written it. Now what about how it will look? I wouldn't want to wake up some day and find a package of galley proofs waiting for me with the whole thing set in Bauhaus Moderne and the chapter numbers spelled out in little snakes.

M: What an imagination! We're glad, in fact overjoyed, to have an author's design suggestions. Hence, you will be consulted, if you wish . . .

J: I wish!

M: But you will not have the final say. If you saw some of the suggestions authors make about typefaces, or their ideas about jacket designs, you'd understand why. I've gotten some cousin's amateur paintings, out-of-focus grey snapshots . . .

J: You'll listen to me seriously—and then you'll do what you want anyway?

M: If you think you're so convincing, why are you worried?

J: To keep designers reasonably happy you can't ride roughshod over them all the time. And they have a tendency to come up with striking designs that don't pay any attention to petty concerns such as whether the type has enough space between lines to be readable. Then if the author gets to see proofs and complains, the reply is that even if the complaints are justified, it's now too expensive to reset.

M: Look, we really will consult you. We'll ask you to give us material for the jacket blurb, too. But you can't design the book.

J: Unless I self-publish it, of course. Let's move along to proofreaders.

M: Even authors have nothing against them. If they're good, they can even save us from residual bits of bad writing and lapses in copy-editing. After the proofs are read by your eagle eyes and a proofreader's, they should be virtually impeccable.

J: That'll be the day. But let's assume the book evades all pitfalls and actually gets printed. How long will this take, incidentally?

M: I like the way you kept your teeth from gnashing when you asked that. It's a good question, and here's the answer: including the editing process, somewhere between eight months and a year.

J: When electronic publishing gets here, it should take about fifteen minutes.

M: *That'll* be the day. In the real world it depends partly on how fast you handle edited manuscript and proofs and the indexing. Authors who've dawdled over a manuscript for five or six years have fits if their publisher's a few days behind schedule with the galley proofs. Then they don't get around to returning the galleys until they're six weeks late. And please keep in mind that publication date is not the same as the date we first receive books in our warehouse, but something like two months later. Besides that, publication date has to fall into one of the two seasons, fall or spring.

J: I thought there were four seasons. In all of which a little friendly drizzle may fall—though I haven't noticed any drops for a while now. Shall we stick our heads out and grab a few pea pods from the hamper to nibble on?

M: Let's. This may feel like summer to you, but in publishing there is no summer, and winter is either the end of fall or the beginning of spring. Anyway, in theory the delay of publication date gives newspapers and magazines time to get reviews assigned and written so they can appear at the official time of publication.

J: I've written book reviews myself and none of this is in contact with reality.

M: No. Bookstores start selling a book whenever they get it. And most reviews don't appear until well after the publication date anyhow—especially in weeklies and monthlies and the journals that review serious books.

J: Then there's the upper-middle-class notion that nobody buys or reads anything from June through August, except "summer reading" at the beach, mysteries and so on. Do you know anybody who spends the summer at the beach reading mysteries?

M: Only my retired aunt, until she died. Actually I'm trying to convince my boss to experiment with publishing some books during the summer, to take advantage of the lessened competition— there's more room on the bookstore shelves. He's afraid people will think we're out of touch with the trade.

J: I'm not liking this boss anymore. He worries too much.

M: You worry too much yourself. Anyway, let's get on to publicity. That *is* something to worry about. We would of course send out proofs for review by trade publications and to get pre-publication blurbs. Do you have friends in high places who'd give you plugs?

J: Only in low and middle places.

M: Well, we'll get them anyhow. We'd send out bales of review copies, with provocative press releases. We'd try to intrigue the media into interviewing you about your wandering retired friends and your unusual view of them. Maybe somebody would send a camera crew to go out with you and film them in their native habitat. We'd help you pull strings behind the scenes to get people with names to pay attention to the book—make it notorious, if we could, since all news *is* good news if they spell your name right. And of course we'd do some ads.

J: Remember my non-negotiable demands.

M: Of course. But you should understand that ads don't really sell middle books. They make authors happy, they may impress other authors and fellow publishers, and they may convince some bookstores to stock books, but they do not have a provable cost-effective impact on sales. The only thing that has a demonstrable effect is direct mail. But we're a general publisher and not set up for a direct-mail operation.

J: So how do you get books into the stores?

M: We have sales reps scouring this country, and also Canada. They're literate and persuasive people, and they're on the road a lot themselves, so they just might conceivably take a fancy to your book and sell surprising quantities of it in advance of publication. When that happens, we begin to hope that once the book hits the stores there will be good word-of-mouth among readers too.

J: There's no way to start word-of-mouth?

M: Not really. You can give away a lot of copies, but it may not work. These things are mysterious, Jim. Some books just seem to strike a live nerve. People pass them around, tell each other about them, give them as gifts. You can see it in their eyes when they talk about them. Other books, maybe far superior from a literary standpoint, somehow never connect with more than a select handful of readers.

J: Some of my writer friends think publishers can create schlock best sellers at will—take a big author name, whether or not the manuscript is any good, spend enough money on hoopla, and force lots of copies into bookstores. Voilà, eighty thousand copies.

M: If that was true, why would publishers ever publish anything but best sellers? You haven't decided we're noble after all, have you?

J: Well, I intend to rely on blind faith in my work's public appeal. After all, isn't *Home on the Road* a comic vision of the human fate?

M: You might say that, if you had a strange sense of humor.

J: I mean in the classic sense of comedy—the opposite of tragedy. People no better than us muddling through, tolerating each other's idiocies, having some fun, bearing up under trouble, not taking life too seriously, surviving . . .

M: All right, I'll push my boss harder. He said yesterday that the next seasonal list isn't really quite full enough. That's a propitious sign.

J: But you don't want to give me false encouragement.

M: Exactly.

J: Actually, Michelle, I wouldn't mind a little encouragement, at this point.

M: Have faith—it'll work out somehow! My advice is to follow the usual rules for unexplored country. Follow Path A until it becomes impassable, at which point you have to back up and take Path B, which in this case is self-publishing. One way or other, you'll get it published. I read you as a man who can get what he wants.

J: But not in a week?

M: Maybe not. I make no promises—except that we have another date for lunch next week. Jim, books can be around for a long while once they're published. Sometimes it's worth waiting for things, you know!

J: I guess that'll have to be encouragement enough. Anyway, I do appreciate your laying all this out.

M: You don't sound that appreciative.

J: Well, I have to confess something, Michelle. I'm having trouble with the idea that *you're* the one who's helping me—or may be helping me. I was always the authority, the one who could send you to the right books, tell you where you had gotten something wrong . . .

M: And now I'm sitting here, setting *you* straight, and it feels uncomfortable. It's even my blanket.

J: Yes. And I don't greatly admire that about myself. I like to think I'm supportive of women in general, and of women in responsible positions in particular. Now you come along, and it's exciting—but a little scary.

M: I'm scary? To you? With your arm around me?

J: Sure. You're in a position of real power. You accept and reject manuscripts and throw these awful numbers around. But no, that isn't really it. It's more personal. You're not respectful, adoring Michelle any more. So I don't quite know how to relate to you. I never know what you're going to do next.

M: Yes, but I don't know what you're going to do next, either. At this point you hardly seem any older than I am. And maybe not much wiser, either, if you'll forgive me. At any rate you're not my safe, predictable professor any more, are you?

J: But I don't know what I am instead. I'm sure of only one thing—that I'm terribly fond of you.

M: Well, I'm terribly fond of you, too. So let's just let things flow along. Come on, let's stand up and get ourselves organized. I do have to get back and finish some letters this afternoon. We'll carry on next week.—Look, the sun's peeking through again!

MENU FIVE

Martini Cocktail   White Wine
Bouillabaisse
Calamari Sauté
Sea Bass with Lemon Sauce
Pasta al Pesto
Zabaglione

M: Well, Jim, you wanted to see where I spend my time. I hope it was worth waiting two weeks for. Not the big fancy office you expected, I'll bet!

J: No, but you don't have to worry about students crouched outside in the corridor the way I do, and you do have a window that opens—rare these days! And that painting is gorgeous, even if it's probably by the guy you used to live with.

M: I like it. I liked him. I'm a loyal type, same as you. Besides, he's famous now, so a museum will want it some day.

J: Being surrounded by all those manuscript boxes does make it kind of comforting. You'll never lack for reading matter. Do you actually read them all?

M: I've gotten to be a rapid skimmer. But some I do read all the way, savoring every word. Like yours, for instance, in case you're wondering.

J: What really surprises me is how homey you've made it, with that big soft chair and the rug.

M: I had to fight for the chair—people thought it looked too comfortable. Even so, my neck and shoulders can get stiff from reading manuscripts or writing memos. Then I do yoga on the rug.

J: Let me feel those shoulders. Uh-oh! Tight and knotty. Here, a little massage might help.

M: Oh, that does feel good. More, more!

J: I assume you close the door when you do yoga. Will anybody misunderstand if they look in and see us doing this?

M: They wouldn't misunderstand at all, I'm afraid.

J: Let's close the door then. Say, that makes it really quiet in here. Relax! Is your yoga a spiritual discipline or just for exercise?

M: It has a spiritual side, but it's mostly a way to keep my body in some kind of limberness. It also sends more blood to the brain, which editors need, don't you agree? Look at this photo of me and my yoga teacher. It took six months of practice to be able to do that position properly.

J: You're limber, all right! I didn't know you could do that.

M: There are a lot of things you don't know about me, Jim.

J: I'm more than willing to learn. I'd probably like them too.

M: I'm sure you'd like some of them. Others—well, I've been told I'm difficult to get along with. For instance, when I'm hungry I turn irascible, so we'd better get some lunch before I snap at you. Come on, let me check out on the in-or-out board.

J: On our way. But I don't find you difficult at all. Even arguing with you is more fun than I've had in years, and everything I know about you so far I enjoy. I know, for example, that you'd like fish today.

M: We'd better go to that seafood place right across the street then, because I *am* going to order fish. I don't want to disappoint you. —No, you're right, I was feeling like it anyway. I hope you haven't begun to think you can read minds.

J: What's wrong with having such a delightful mind read? —Hey, you're blushing!

M: All right, what's in my mind right now?

J: That's easy . . . you, uh, you feel that these lunches could go on forever. I'm projecting, of course.

M: Close enough. Here we are. Look, a table in the corner!

J: Yes. After many a detour we arrive back in proper publisher's lunch territory, with a literate waitperson, a menu free of gross spelling errors, and honest, healthy neo-peasant cooking—look at the calamari sauté that woman's eating! I have to have that.

M: I'm going to have to start out with a cup of bouillabaisse. They make it wonderfully spicy here. And they do great things to sea bass.

J: Ah, that air laden with basil fumes!

M: Did you notice the artfully arranged mountain of fruit at the door.

J: A festive place altogether. Well, is this a celebration? I'm hoping we can indulge in a bottle of champagne. Have we passed the final exam? Or do we have to deal with more case studies of publishing folly?

M: I have some good news for you, Jim. The reason I put this lunch off a week was to wait for reports from my outside readers, and they're quite positive. The gerontologist finds your manuscript very suggestive as field work, even though she disagrees with your political perspective and wonders why you haven't discussed the latest academic theories. But my retired engineer wants to buy six copies for his friends, and a bookstore owner I talked with thinks he could sell a fair number of copies.

J: Wonderful! Does that mean you have a contract rolled up in your purse there?

M: No, because there's a little bad news too. Not about folly, only delay. Almost everything in publishing can easily get delayed. For instance, my boss had to be out of town for four days and then he was working with our lawyer on a nasty potential libel problem. So he still hasn't gotten to your manuscript, but he wants a look before I go any further with it.

J: Aaaarghhh! You're playing with my sanity, woman!

M: Take it easy . . .

J: I can see the headline: "Irate Author Slays Publisher, Alleges Mental Torture by Inexplicable Delays."

M: They're perfectly explicable.

J: But not forgivable.

M: Aren't you the least bit grateful?

J: Sure, the prisoner is grateful that the hangman's platform doesn't shimmy. But you know what, I'm hardly even surprised. Maybe I'm getting used to publishing. Or immunized. Anyway I guess I'll have to heave a sigh of well-justified resignation and get back to my vows of self-publishing.

M: What? When we have quite a strong case now for Terra doing it?

J: Just tell that boss of yours that it's too late—return the manuscript, and I'll wait to see him squirm when it sells fifty thousand copies! In fact I had suspected something like this would happen, and after lunch I'm going to take a duplicate manuscript to my copy editor and set her to work. I can't stand this any more!

M: Oh, no! Give us just a little more rope . . .

J: Look, for your boss I may be a low priority, but for myself I'm a high priority! So if I don't want to be kicked around, I'm going to go ahead.

M: Jim, I can see why you're so angry. I agree with you—he should have gotten to it. But I want to go on record as saying that it would really be dumb to take your manuscript back at this point.

J: Okay, and I go on record as recognizing that you've done your best, Michelle. Don't look so worried, it's not the end of the world. I think self-publishing is going to be a great adventure. Think of all the consultation we can do as I stumble along through it. In fact, why don't we celebrate my entry into the publishing madness by getting good and drunk and having a wonderful lunch?

M: That's the first rational thing you've said so far today. I'm for it. Shall we go back to martinis?

J: An excellent idea! You know, I finally *am* beginning to understand publishers. For a while I thought there must be some mysterious inherent contradiction between editorial talent and managerial ability . . .

M: Thanks a whole lot!

J: But no, the problem is that in a business where every product is unique and often troublesome and takes special talents to produce and sell, you can't really get anything down to a sensible fixed system. It's an artisan occupation, like something in the Middle Ages. So it ought to be done by small, closely integrated teams who learn how to work together smoothly, something like a European movie crew.

M: But they're just making one film, and then they take a vacation to recover from it.

J: You're missing the point. In a human-scale operation you don't need inter-office memos, you don't have inter-departmental power struggles, you just settle things over a cup of coffee. But that can't be done in a company of thirty or forty people, much less eighty, with the work split up by departments. That simply can't be coordinated. There can't possibly be anybody effectively in charge—because if there were, they would only screw it up still worse. So it's one industry where creative anarchism is the only answer.

M: I doubt if that would pay the bills. But you're not

accusing us of terminal incompetence after all?

J: Not personally, no. It's the *institution* that's incompetent, the way it's presently organized. That explains why, when authors get together and exchange publishing experiences, we find that incompetence is spread around with such marvelous evenness.

M: I don't like that smug grin. We're stuck in this together, aren't we?

J: Of course, that's what makes it a comedy. If the comedian could walk around the banana peel, there wouldn't be any joke.

M: Well, I'm not laughing, just drinking. But listen, there's another factor too. Because salaries aren't terribly good, especially on the lower levels, jobs in publishing tend to be like musical chairs. People keep moving around in order to edge up the scale, leaving their messes behind them.

J: I hope *you're* not thinking of going somewhere else!

M: Not me. I'm only doing gallows sociology, like you.

J: Okay, here's another theory I had about the musical chairs—that editors are easily bored.

M: Well, maybe we're spoiled by having new authors and manuscripts to deal with all the time. So we look for new companies too. Of course this has the unfortunate result that books get marooned when the editor who signed them up is no longer there.

J: Here, if we're going to be so stoical, let's have another round. Don't the authors sue, or something? Are their agents still sleeping off the hangovers they acquired with the advance money?

M: It can take a long time to tell whether things have really gone off the track. Sometimes publishers will hear of a competing book in the works, and try to hold off paying the final chunk of the advance until they can tell whether they really want to do your book. But authors and agents are like editors and everybody else—they keep hoping for the best. Suing is expensive and slow, and besides you may lose.

J: But surely an author can make a publisher produce or get off the pot?

M: We can always say the manuscript is not "satisfactory in form and content" in some way or other, and you'd have to prove it is. I could make a list of twenty things gravely wrong with *Home on the Road,* if I had to.

J: That's a sinister little smile—I'll *bet* you could! But when delays get really ghastly, why don't publishers just send the manuscripts back and let the authors find another publisher? I heard of one guy whose book took four years to get out. After that he became an agent, so he could stick it to publishers with other people's books. Hah!

M: Don't be mean. Delays usually arise just from confusion and procrastination, or occasionally from a shortage of capital to pay printers. Of course there's sometimes a clause in the contract that defines what "publishing within a reasonable time" will mean—that's the usual boiler-plate phrase. You can set a fixed number of months from delivery of the manuscript or from its acceptance.

J: And how is it legally established when the clock starts running?

M: Hey, you're getting sharp, aren't you? Here's to you, Jim. A promising student if I ever saw one.

J: Just a damn minute, here. Let's not get too carried away with this role reversal stuff!

M: Excuse *me*. I thought I was making a little joke—don't be so touchy!

J: Maybe I want to be touchy. I'm on dangerous ground here.

M: No, you're not, but you can't see that yet. Anyway—normally you'd get the last installment of the advance. Or else there should be an official acceptance letter. If a publisher doesn't write one, just phones, a wise author should get a letter as soon as possible.

J: And publishers actually live up to these time limit clauses?

M: Well, I wouldn't want to have plowed money into editing and design and typesetting and then have an author yank the project out from under me. But when you're that far along, most authors would stay with you even if you run a couple of months late, rather than have to try to find another publisher and lose a year by going through the whole routine again.

J: Maybe they should just demand ransom. Or rather rent, for the privilege of sitting on the manuscript. You know, I'm quite crocked, and you're looking unbelievably lovely. Why don't we just run away together? Why are we talking about all this stupid business?

M: Because I don't dare stop. At least until I've drunk a couple more glasses of wine. Besides I couldn't abandon my sea bass, which is exquisite with this lemony sauce.

J: All right, I'll have to console myself with a little side order of pasta al pesto.

M: Come to think of it, there *is* a possibility here: the contract could specify that for every three months of delay in publishing, beyond a year, the royalty scale jumps up a point or at least an additional advance is due. That would keep the question from snowballing into an all-or-nothing affair. It would give the publisher a graduated incentive to get the book out, or else to drop it cleanly. Though that might mean sacrificing the advance if there was one, or at least waiting to get the money back, if it was a returnable advance.

J: I'd better try to pull myself together here. You mean the publisher would have to pay the author cash for the publisher's delays? I *like* that!

M: Publishers wouldn't like it.

J: Sure, but if a publisher refused the clause it would show they weren't serious about getting the book out promptly, and I'd rather know that up front so I could find another publisher. Would you put it in a contract with one of *your* authors? Me, for example?

M: For you, yes. For others, I wouldn't exactly volunteer it, but I could live with it, I guess—I just thought it up, after all. Here's to my unquenchable generosity!

J: Hey, I thought it was *my* idea. I ought to pass it on to

the National Writers Union. They're always looking for
new ways to save authors from shark-toothed publishers.

M: What? Are you a member of that outfit? I've been giving
away trade secrets to a union spy?

J: Sure, you've been fraternizing with the enemy.

M: Never an enemy. Maybe misguided, that's all.

J: Let's drink to friendly emenies—I mean enemies. Here's
to people who challenge us, throw us off stride, make
us think.

M: All right, but frankly I've gotten along fine so far without seeing too much of the Writers Union.

J: I wasn't just talking about the Union.

M: I know, but I don't want *you* as an enemy, either. I just
want you to keep on looking at me with that inebriated
fascination. But go ahead and tell me more about the Union.
What can it do for writers that a decent agent can't?

J: It organizes meetings where we can hold each others'
hands and warn each other about publishers, and that makes
writing less lonely work. It has an informative newsletter
and it can hold press conferences to get into the media.
And look what happens when some sleazy magazine's
headed for Chapter Eleven. They've paid their rent, their
light-bill, their printers, their mailing service—but they
won't answer their writers' phone calls. Then Union at-
torneys threaten to sue, and somehow money turns up.
Agents can't get tough that way. They spend too much
time in bed with publishers.

M: I don't even let them call me Baby.—Now who's blushing?

J: I just realized you might think I meant that you . . .

M: I appreciate your *délicatesse*. I wouldn't know myself, of course, but I've been told that agents and publishers and even authors have been suspected of going to bed together, on occasion—in any combination of genders. Probably after a lot of drinks at a publisher's lunch.

J: Maybe they slide under the table and do it there. But they'd need a bigger table than this.

M: We're safe then. But seriously, you're right. Let's see, what were you right about? Oh, yes, an individual author *is* rarely as important to an agent as the publishers the agent has to deal with over the long haul.

J: That's another reason why authors need more checks and balances. Besides, the Union can use its media access to raise issues in a way that individual writers might be ashamed or ill-advised to. I don't think publishers enjoy having unsavory practices advertised to the writing community. So I gather they're a little more careful because the Union exists. Sometimes they even try to look generous, like by extending their libel-liability insurance coverage to the writers they publish, because they know it'll win points with writers.

M: Baloney. Publishers did that out of good will, and to simplify the legal ramifications.

J: No, they suddenly realized it didn't actually cost them anything extra in premiums. That's a good definition of publisher generosity—giving something away that doesn't cost them anything.

M: Well, in my experience writers are so jealous and spiteful about each other's successes that it'd be a major miracle if they could sustain a strong union. They're the ultimate American individualists. They believe solely in themselves, blind luck, and the universal recognition they're sure they personally deserve. So anything called a union would seem just too, too working-class.

J: You're wrong there. Wrong, wrong. More and more writers understand they're hired hands. And underpaid at that. They're more disillusioned than the Authors Guild assumes. Not that something called a guild can't be militant —look at the strikes of the Hollywood guilds.

M: I admit that the Authors Guild worked out an intelligent ideal contract, from an author's point of view. I hate to see the damned things coming.

J: And they have a newsletter full of grisly facts. They can also be fairly tough, in a genteel way. I'm a Guild member too, one of the members who keep their average-income tables so low. It was through the Guild I learned that unless your contract says otherwise, foreign rights income or paperback income won't be passed through when it arrives, but gets held until your next royalty payment, which usually comes four months after the actual calendar sales period ends. You wouldn't do that to me, would you?

M: Not if you can get us to say otherwise in the contract. Unless you do, with luck in the timing we might be able to hang onto your money for most of a year.

J: You call it luck, I call it theft! At least I could ask for interest. On late royalty payments, too. One author figures that his big New York publisher raises its profits and costs its authors something in the six figures every year, just by being consistently about a month late in sending out checks.

M: Sure, ask. Here's to asking, without which one doth not receive. You want to know something you should try to eliminate from a contract? Watch for a clause saying that if you've published one book with a publisher, and it hasn't earned back its advance, the earnings of a new book with that same publisher may be applied against that unearned old advance, before anything is applied against the new advance. It can be a long time before you see any more money. They call it cross-collateralization. I call it chicanery, myself.

J: A fine term, chicanery. We don't hear that term enough anymore.—Hey, which side are you on, here? Are you so sloshed you can actually agree with an author?

M: I'm on the side of truth. Can't we both be on that side, my Jim?

J: Let's try, but it may not be easy. Anyway, I want my books to be kept un-cross-whatever-you-call-it. And if I can't get that—well, it sounds like another way to motivate authors to switch publishers after every book, or try self-publishing. As if there weren't enough motivations already.

M: True. Though sometimes I might think an author *should* be penalized for having an agent who twisted the publisher's arm unreasonably.

J: At least if I were a self-publisher I wouldn't have to

worry about funny accounting. And I'd never, never be mad at my publisher.

M: If I'm your publisher, you're not going to be mad at me.

J: My beautiful dreamer! Remember how I used to chew you out about your papers?

M: You'd yell at me for not living up to my own standards. It was never you against me. It was us together, against laziness and inattention. That's what I want for us again. You know, Jim, what really appeals to me about being a publisher is precisely that experience of all-out shared effort. We'd be working together to make the manuscript into the most absolutely powerful, tight, funny, troubling book possible. I'd be giving you tough feedback, cheering you on, helping you with whatever wisdom I've accumulated over the years . . .

J: Sounds like you'd be *my* teacher now.

M: Well, I suppose editing *is* a kind of teaching, a very collaborative, creative kind. I love it when it goes well—it's really an intimate process, you know.

J: I'm for that, even if I'd have to learn more new turnabouts in our relationship.

M: Here's to turnabouts, then—you can do it, Jim! And I'd be scheming and conniving to get the designer and printers to produce the most beautiful book you could imagine. And we'd work with the sales and promotion people to make the biggest splash conceivable. It's so gratifying when it all goes together like that! Wouldn't self-publishing be awfully lonely, by contrast?

J: Well, I find my own company acceptable, but what you're really saying is that we could be partners?

M: Hey, you've got it at last! A toast—to the new Jim!

J: All right, so I've been a slow learner about all this. I'm grateful for your tolerance, Michelle.

M: Emotional lessons are harder to learn than intellectual ones.

J: You bet. So we could be equals, huh? I'm beginning to like the feel of that.—It was easy for me to grasp that you're at least as bright as I am. I first realized it when you did a paper on the logical problems in the concept of contradiction.

M: You remember that?

J: Sure. Now some academic has finally written a whole book on the subject. And remember that time in class you said that Plato hadn't progressed beyond confusing the word with the thing, and that Socrates was guilty of faulty logic? You took it personally—you got quite cross. I think that was when I first realized you were somebody to reckon with.

M: It offended my sense of drama that his friends let Socrates get away with slippery slides in his terms. Such pushovers! Later I discovered that words and things aren't that easy to separate. And also that Plato could have used a good editor.

J: He was probably a misguided self-publisher.—You know something? I'm about to surprise you, I hope. You make working together sound so attractive that I've decided

I *can* stand the pain of waiting a little longer to see whether your blessed boss will let you draw me as a wild card. Just promise one thing, though—we'll have another lunch whether he's made up his mind or not. Let's face it, he could take weeks. Months!

M: Oh, thank you, Jim! Thanks so much! I promise you it won't be long now. Of course we'll have our lunch—I'm already counting on it. And I *am* surprised. I know it isn't easy for you to be patient.

J: When you look at me like that, I . . . listen, why do we have to wait till next week to see each other again? How about dinner tomorrow? Or the day after, or the day after that?

M: No. That would be mixing more pleasure with business than I'm capable of. At the moment, anyway.

J: You *are* difficult. Is that why you're not involved with anybody?

M: Maybe. I keep hoping to be appreciated for the ways I'm difficult.

J: I can't imagine you go unappreciated.

M: Oh, there are plenty of men around. "Successful" men, endearing bums, sweet guys who're married but don't tell me about it until it's too late. Then there are the lesbians who feel I've never discovered my true sexuality. But appreciation, real appreciation . . .

J: I know what you mean. Even out where I live, there are plenty of lovely women. Since the divorce I haven't been lacking for company, but I haven't met anybody I could take seriously, you know what I mean?

M: Here, refill my glass, will you? It's enough to drive a person to celibacy. Or drink.

J: Not me. I've been making up for lost time. And trying to pay enough attention to get some idea of what women want.

M: Really?

J: I hope! A glimmer, anyway.

M: Well, one thing I've discovered is that sex can be friendly. It doesn't always have to involve neurotic longing and doubt and anguish, all that romantic poetic stuff. Of course now we've got AIDS tests and safe sex, so it's hard to fall into that old romantic swoon even if you wanted to.

J: I just did the AIDS test. It felt like taking out a life-insurance policy.

M: That's funny, so did I . . . to remove any lurking anxieties.

J: Hey, look at us, we've both survived the sexual revolution!—Actually I don't mind a certain amount of swooning so long as I remember that it's a matter of romantic comedy. Underneath, though, I'm still a diehard romantic. I know Ms. Right is around somewhere, waiting for me.

M: Oh, come on.

J: No, I've had to admit it. I really do want a girl next door, someone that I can feel easy about disagreeing with sometimes. She sings in her morning shower. She understands my cynicism and thinks it's funny—and she also knows that I don't entirely mean it, and that a lot of it comes from my feelings being tender. She's the kind of person who sees that life is not a bowl of cherries but always turns up something good on the menu anyway.

M: Well, if that's what you want, I . . .

J: Yes?

M: What was I saying, anyway? How much of this have we drunk? And how much marsala did they put in the zabaglione? I just meant I'm sure there should be plenty of applicants. At least four or five—out of the two and a half billion women on earth now.

J: So who knows, maybe at this moment Ms. Right is sitting in this very restaurant. Maybe just over there . . .

M: Where? I'll poke her eyes out! She's not *really* right for you.

J: You know who's right for me?

M: Dear Jim.—What an expression on your face!

J: I've never had to deal with such a beautiful woman holding my heart in her hands before. Here, close them up gently.

M: Jim, remember this is a publisher's lunch.

J: I'll kiss you on your editorial ear, then.

M: Isn't a hand enough for you?

J: No. Not nearly enough.

M: Well, in that case—I wouldn't let any other author do this, you know.

J: Yes, I know.

6

MENU SIX

Coffee

M: Hi! I'm really glad you could come over, Jim.

J: You don't look like you're exactly at death's door. In fact you look like your usual radiant self. What have you got, anyway?

M: I don't know, maybe nothing. I woke up with a head-ache, decided to pamper myself—make a caffe latte, take a nice long bath, spend the morning catching up on reading some manuscripts. So I called in to say I was working at home today. One of the great things about editorial work is that you can do it anywhere.

J: Even in the bathtub?

M: It can be done, but I tend to doze off. Want to see one of my secret luxuries?

J: Sure, show me everything. I'm curious to see how you live these days. You've come a long way from our crummy dormitories!

M: Take a good look, then. The kitchen's in here—this is where I actually spend most of my time. It's a good big space, with a table for reading on and making notes—not too much sun, and a tree to look out at.

J: I like the couch too. Every kitchen should have one. And evidently your interest in food isn't limited to eating in restaurants—did you publish any of these cookbooks?

M: Not personally, but there should be a Terra title in there somewhere about food in the future. Basically, we'll all be eating Chinese. Over here's the bedroom.

J: Where did you get that gorgeous kimono on the wall? Isn't that a wisteria pattern?

M: Yes—quite rare, actually. It's a wedding kimono. Japanese brides only wear them once, so you can get them cheap in secondhand stores in Kyoto.

J: I wonder about the deep significance of a wedding kimono in the bedroom of an unwed damsel.

M: I wouldn't agonize over it, if I were you. Now for the high point of the tour. Take a look at this: it's a special Japanese soaking tub. The water comes right up to your neck. There's insulation inside to keep the water hot for a long time. Here's my back-scratching sponge. I like lots of great big towels. And I've even got a teeny view—I had a friend knock out a piece of wall to make that window for me.

J: I like this sybaritic side! It rather changes my fantasies about you.

M: You had me taking cold showers and bouncing on a trampoline?

J: No. If you really want to know, my fantasies about you start with your eyes. Oh, Michelle, I've always . . .

M: Wait, wait—don't say it. I've got to tell you something.

J: Yes? Why are you looking down at the floor like that?

M: We're not going to publish your book.

J: So that's it, eh? You and your wild card books! You and your great boss! You and your noble publishing house!

M: Jim, look . . .

J: Oh, you talk a civilized and cultivated game, but when it comes down to it you people would rather not do anything that isn't a sure shot! Michelle, you were the bravest and the clearest of all the students I've ever had, but now you cave in and bow down to the dollar like everybody else. You don't care about ideas, you don't even care about the country. You're a bunch of money grubbers, just like the worst of them in New York! Who owns this fancy Terra outfit now anyway, Dow Chemical? Gulf & Western?

M: Jim, just a minute . . .

J: *You* wait a minute! You think authors aren't onto all this? We know you're all heartless. You diddle around with me, tantalize me, then toss me on the junkpile! But always sweetly reasonable—"Oh yes, Jim, you're such a good man and I'm terribly fond of you." But then it turns out that the book I sweated my life's blood on is just too difficult for you—you have to get on with your next goddamned cat book. Why do you people keep pretending you have something to do with *culture*? Give me back my manuscript, I'm getting out of here, you, you miserable *publisher*!

M: Oh no, you're not. Get away from that door! You're so hot for truth, okay, I'll give you some, about authors!

You write books that nobody wants and then wonder why your publishers can't sell them to the movies for seven figures. You don't have the faintest notion of what goes on in bookstores—or in a publisher's warehouse when the returns of your marvelous brainchildren come flooding back. You never had to meet a payroll, you just expect some publisher daddy or mommy figure to keep sending you checks because you're cute and in love with your pitiful little patty-cake pile of semi-original shit. You don't meet deadlines, you reserve your greatest creativity for explaining away your own failures. Then you think that some miraculous new technology is going to enable you to do it all for yourselves. Well, good luck, suckers! You're just a pack of abominable, narcissistic, self-indulgent, know-it-all assholes! Go self-publish and be damned! And *now* you can get out of here!

J: Michelle, I love you!

M: What? What are you doing? Get away . . .

J: I love you. Come here, come here—kiss me . . .

M: Oh yes, mmmmm! Yes, hold me tighter! Oh Jim, where have you been so long? Oh, let's get closer! Mmmmm. I think I've loved you ever since I saw you ambling up to the front of that first lecture hall.

J: And I've loved you since the instant I laid eyes on you, sitting there with such sweet expectation on your face. Besides that, you've got such a delicious feel . . .

M: Kiss me again, like that. Mmmmmmmmmm!

J: I didn't dare admit it, but ever since you disappeared I

couldn't stop fantasizing about getting you back into bed again. And again, and again. You're like some kind of wonderful ripening fruit, filling up that beautiful skin— mmmmmMMM! How can you be so smart and such fun and so desirable all at the same time?

M: Jim, oh Jim, such loving hands! It's always just felt so good to be around you. I'd watch those hands, but I could hardly let myself think—oh, God, come into my bedroom, I love you, you adorable man!

J: Can we bear to stop talking?

M: Just barely.

J: I think seeing you bare may totally blow out my verbal circuits.

M: Let's dare to be bare. Mmmm, take that off, oh yes!

✳ ✳ ✳

M: Jim, Jim. How sweet you look, all drowsy from love.

J: My love is like a pink, pink rose. Her eyes are droopy next her nose . . .

M: And on the floor her scattered clothes . . .

J: Cover like leaves all former woes . . .

M: Reminding her that now she knows . . .

J: He loves her, loves her, head to toes.

M: What a fantastic feeling to have you *really* in my life!

J: Make room, dear Michelle, I thrash around a lot.

M: You know I can handle that. I think we can handle *anything*. What an adventure this is going to be! Having you around will make me a better publisher, you know. Maybe we can even set up our own publishing company some day. How would you like *that*?

J: I'd like it a lot, because *then* maybe you'd finally publish my book!

M: I certainly would. Besides—well, now I have to confess something.

J: What? This had better be good. You have a hard act to follow.

M: You're telling me. Okay, here it is: in all our lunches, I kept to our bargain. I told you truthfully about publishing, right on the line, a lot of the bitter along with the sweet. But today, I lied to you about something.

J: I hope all you mean is that I'm not going to get the coffee you promised when you lured me over here.

M: What I mean is, we *do* want to publish your book. In fact I have the contract in the kitchen, waiting for your signature.

J: You do? What—well, that's—wait a minute, Michelle, what's going on? Why did you tell me that you were rejecting the book? What am I supposed to believe here?

M: Do you remember what I said about not being able to mix too much pleasure with business? Of course I've wanted to go to bed with you all along. Last week when we got smashed together I almost died at having to put you off. It would have been so easy, and so natural, after wanting each other so long! But it would have been taking a big risk.

J: Sounds to me like a risk worth taking.

M: Listen carefully. Suppose I had said that Terra was going to publish the book, and you were grateful and happy, and after that we got involved. You might have always secretly suspected that I'd decided to publish your book as part of a deep dark plot to win you. And if we had made love before the decision, I might have always suspected that you'd wanted to get me into bed again partly to entice me into publishing your book. But now we're clear and clean. Your love for me came through so strongly, Jim, even when you thought I wouldn't publish the book! Not to mention after hearing me say all those dreadful things.

J: Well, most of them were true, after all.

M: Yes, but I've also known some authors who were kind and good and talented and modest. Besides you, of course. I indulged in a bit of overkill there, I'm afraid.

J: But I had said some pretty terrible things myself. Not all entirely true either, of course—I guess I should admit that I do know of a *few* books that were well and properly published. But let me get this clear: you were testing me, is that it?

M: And you passed the final with a double A plus! —You aren't mad about the deception?

J: Considering the denouement, not at all. Besides, turn-about *is* fair play. My incomparable Michelle—several steps ahead of me, as usual!

M: Isn't it comforting that we've known each other so long? Even if you *are* an author, I've always felt I could trust you.

J: Perhaps, but look at it from my end, my darling. You may be my love forever, but all this proves my point: never altogether trust a publisher. I'll sign your contract, but there *will* be trouble ahead—we'll just have to learn to enjoy it. So let's not get totally carried away. I'll have to stay abreast of the latest wiles of self-publishing, so I always have a fall-back position— and also to keep you honest. In fact, I reserve the right to hate you as a publisher, let's say on alternate Thursdays, even though I love you to distraction the rest of the time.

M: We'll have to see. That sounds like a heavy negotiation. Maybe another three or four lunches' worth?

J: If we concentrated. Naked lunches?

M: Mmmm!

J: And now *I* have a confession to make. I've been secretly tape-recording our lunches.

M: You rat! You mean *all* our lunches—including this one? You've bugged my bedroom?

J: I bugged my tweedy old jacket, actually. The one on the floor over there.

M: Double rat! I take everything back. Get your hands off me! I'll . . .

J: Oh no, you don't. Remember, once a publisher, always a publisher! So just consider this—the tapes will make an interesting little publishing project. I'll transcribe them, we'll do a bit of editing, and there we have it—*My Lunches with Michelle.* I can see a movie deal already. Come on, unclench that fist.

M: Well, you know—maybe you have something there after all. But in my professional judgment it'll take a *lot* of editing. Short books are best, is my motto. And we can do better than that title.

J: Oh, yeah?

M: Yeah. Why not *Publisher's Lunch?*

T H E   E N D

APPENDIX

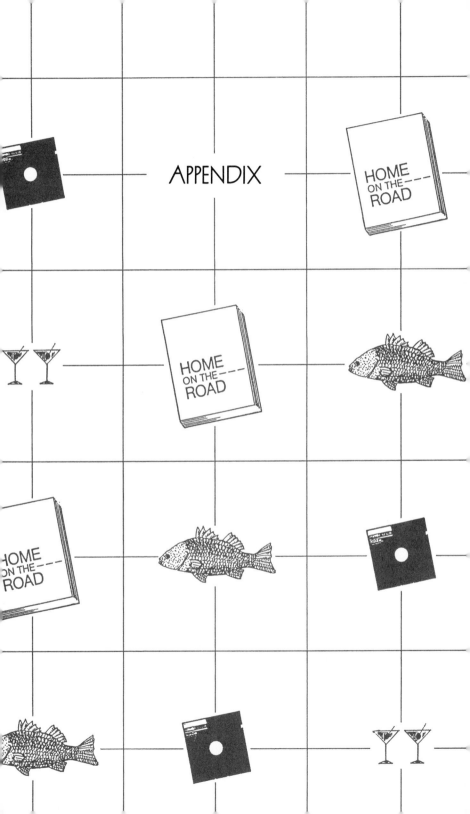

Authors Guild, 234 West 44th Street, New York, NY 10035, tel. (212) 398-0838. Guild members can obtain a model contract form. The Guild publishes an excellent newsletter.

National Writers Union, 13 Astor Place, New York, NY 10003, tel. (212) 254-0279. NWU members can obtain a booklet, "Fifteen Points to a Better Contract," and a model contract form. The NWU publishes a newletter and occasional bulletins, maintains a data bank on how publishers treat writers, and operates a grievance system.

FOR FURTHER INFORMATION
ABOUT PUBLISHING:

How to Get Happily Published, by Judith Applebaum and Nancy Evans. NAL Penguin, 120 Woodbine St., Bergenfield, NJ 07621, tel. (800) 526-0275.

Literary Agents: How to Get & Work with the Right One for You, by Michael Larsen. Writer's Digest Books, 1507 Dana Avenue, Cincinnati, OH 45207, tel. (800) 543-4644.

Handbook for Academic Authors, by Beth Luey. Cambridge University Press, 32 East 57th Street, New York, NY 10022, tel. (800) 688-8888.

Publishers Weekly. R. R. Bowker Co., P.O. Box 13731, Philadelphia, PA 19101. The main trade journal; expensive, but available in most libraries.

The Writer. 120 Boylston Street, Boston MA 02116. This magazine also publishes *The Writer's Handbook*, a useful annual volume.

Writer's Digest. 1507 Dana Avenue, Cincinnati, OH 45207, tel. (800) 543-4644. Also publishes *Writer's Market*, a yearly compendium of market information. (Now in separate volume: *Fiction Writer's Market.*)

The Writer's Legal Companion, by Brad Bunnin & Peter Beren. Addison-Wesley, 1 Jacob Way, Reading, MA 01867, tel. (800) 447-2226.

FOR INFORMATION ABOUT SELF-PUBLISHING:

The Self-Publishing Manual, by Dan Poynter. Para Publishing, P.O. Box 4232-804, Santa Barbara, CA 93140-4232, tel. (805) 968-7277.

Complete Guide to Self-Publishing, by Tom and Marilyn Ross. Writer's Digest Books, 1507 Dana Avenue, Cincinnati, OH 45207, tel. (800) 543-4644.

FOR HELP IN SELLING BOOKS THAT HAVE GONE OUT OF PRINT:

Buckley-Little Book Catalog, 19 West 36th Street, 12th floor, New York, NY 10018, tel. (212) 307-1300.

INDEX TO PUBLISHING TERMS

COLOPHON
(OR A NOTE ON THIS BOOK)

The text of *Publisher's Lunch* was written using WordStar on a Kaypro IBM-PC clone. The author received bountiful bolstering from Dorothy Bryant, Catherine Campbell, Toni Ihara, Richard Kahlenberg, Richard Lucas, Celeste MacLeod, Carole Malkin, Malcolm Margolin, Danny Moses, Charlotte Painter, Michael Phillips, Steve Rice, Randee Russell, and most of all Christine Leefeldt and Jake Warner. But despite help from these and other wonderful friends, not to mention the miracles of word-processing technology, it still took him three years to complete his work—or about an eighth of a page per day. The manuscript then sat on desks at Ten Speed for a couple of months, after which it was the subject of a most amicable publisher's lunch with George Young and Phil Wood at Christopher's Cafe in Berkeley; the author consumed a fashionably underdone piece of albacore and accepted a modest advance on condition that the contract would incorporate the innovative terms Jim asks for in the text. Sal Glynn oversaw the project for Ten Speed, catching the author napping at various points, contributing ingenious ideas, and making sure the editorial corrections were entered correctly. Nancy Austin designed and illustrated the cover and interior of the book, The Compleat Works typeset the pages in 11/13 Stemple Garamond from the author's disk, and Malloy Lithographing, Inc. did the printing and binding. The rest, dear reader, is up to you.